The Stone That Spoke

A French general dreams of a new world empire and invades Egypt. A British diplomat has himself lowered down the face of a mountain to copy inscriptions. A German schoolteacher makes a bet, and an eleven-year-old makes a vow. Findings that inspire the work of countless scholars are made by a doctor, an architect, and a banknote engraver. The discovery and decipherment of lost languages are the story of men like Champollion, Rawlinson, and Ventris. They are the clues that pointed to whole civilizations forgotten and lost in the passing of centuries. In this absorbing book one learns how the decipherers, amateur and expert alike, have contributed enormously to the knowledge gained by the science of archaeology.

The Rosetta Stone, Clue to the Hieroglyphs

The Stone That Spoke

And Other Clues To
The Decipherment
Of Lost Languages

by Steven Frimmer

G. P. Putnam's Sons   New York

For Barbara

J
417
F

CONTENTS

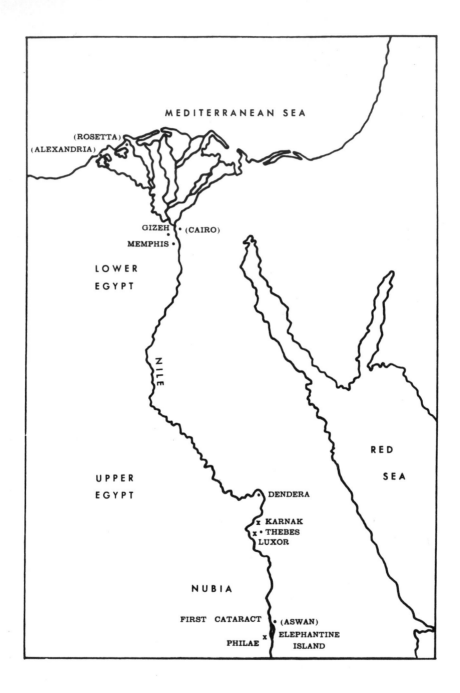

MEDITERRANEAN SEA

(ROSETTA)
(ALEXANDRIA)

GIZEH
• (CAIRO)
MEMPHIS •

LOWER

EGYPT

NILE

RED

SEA

UPPER

EGYPT

• DENDERA

x KARNAK
x • THEBES
LUXOR

NUBIA

FIRST CATARACT   • (ASWAN)
PHILAE x   ELEPHANTINE
            ISLAND

Chapter One

Land of Mystery

I

Gazing out across the sands of the Egyptian desert, a sentinel has squatted for thousands of years. A silent monster, part man and part beast, he guards the relics of a long-dead civilization. The Sphinx is one of the oldest and most familiar monuments in mankind's long history, but we know very little about him. He is a symbol of what Egypt was for centuries—a land of mystery.

The Great Sphinx of Gizeh, to give him his proper name, is the largest piece of sculpture that has survived from ancient times. The head and forepart of the body were hewed out of a single piece of living rock 66 feet high. The body, which is that of a lion, measures slightly more than 240 feet from claws to tail. The paws and most of the body are made of brick. The head, a human head, has a face more than 13 feet wide.

What little we know about the Sphinx and what has been done to him by time and man represent, in brief, the story of the rediscovery of Egypt. He has been buried and unburied, damaged and repaired, measured, studied, and pictured endlessly. His story has been reconstructed painstakingly by scholars but remains part legend. He links the present with the dimmest past but, through all the centuries, has kept some of his secrets to himself.

A misconception identifying him with the monster, half beast, half woman, in the Greek story of Oedipus, gave the Sphinx his name. The ancient Egyptians considered him the embodiment of Harmakhis (Hamarchis), the sun-god, and his face may be a portrait of Khafre, the king who ruled when the massive statue was carved. An ancient Egyptian text gives us some clue to the statue's great age. A young prince, says the text, napped one day in the shade of the Sphinx. As he slept, the statue spoke to him, promising him Egypt's throne if he would clear away the sand. This he did, and the prophecy was fulfilled, for the prince became Thutmose IV. We know that he ruled 3,400 years ago, and the text tells us that the Sphinx, at that time, was already 1,100 years old.

Along with the Sphinx, other wonders mark the existence of a once-great civilization that flourished on the banks of the Nile thousands of years ago. Travelers in Egypt for centuries reported on and marveled at the more than sixty pyramids, the largest one hundreds of

8

feet high and containing 2,500,000 blocks of stone. And there were magnificent temples, with exotic wall paintings, and enormous statues, most of them half-buried in the sand. But like the Sphinx, all these wonders remained, from classical times to the beginning of the nineteenth century, mysteries that defied explanation.

Perhaps most mysterious of all was the fact that many of these wonders, particularly the obelisks—pointed columns of stone rising as high as 90 feet—were covered with strange decorative inscriptions. These inscriptions were called hieroglyphics from the Greek word meaning sacred carvings. Most of the people familiar with these hieroglyphics believed them to be some form of writing, but nobody could decipher their meaning, nobody could translate them. When scientific study of this ancient writing began, hieroglyphics was a lost and forgotten language that had last been used 1,400 years earlier.

II

What most people knew of ancient Egypt was what Herodotus had written about it in the fifth century B.C. Herodotus, who is often called the Father of History, spent many years traveling thousands of miles through Greece, Asia Minor, and the eastern Mediterranean. He traveled east to such fabled cities as Babylon and Susa, up the west coast of the Black Sea to the mouth of the Dnieper River, and south to Egypt, where he made a long visit. His famous *Histories* were written and polished in the last years before his death in 425 B.C. The *Histories* are traditionally divided into nine books, named for the Muses, and it is the second book that is devoted to Egypt.

Not only was Herodotus the principal source of information about Egypt, but he was also the source of many misconceptions. Facts and fictions, pertinent observations and incredible fancies stand side by side in his great work. He established, for a hundred generations to come, the prevailing notions about Egypt.

His most famous statement about Egypt, that it was "a gift of the river Nile," was his most perceptive. He wondered about the cause of the Nile's annual flooding, but he rejected the true reason as too unbelievable and stated flatly that the source of the river was an inexplicable mystery. Herodotus was aware of Egypt's great age, calling it the second oldest nation, and described its marvels in great detail. Of the Pyramid of Cheops he wrote that it took 100,000 men twenty years to build, and he said it measured 800 feet wide by 800 feet high and was made of stone blocks 30 feet or more in length. These exaggerated figures were accepted by countless readers who rejected his less precisely stated fancies.

The study of hieroglyphics was hampered for centuries by his misconceptions. His statement "They have two sorts of writing, one called sacred and the other common" gave rise to the false theory that hieroglyphic writing was used only for religious purposes. More important, he spoke of hieroglyphics as picture writing,

10

establishing the notion that each symbol represented a specific word. The long struggle to decipher hieroglyphics is based on this misconception, and the key to decipherment was discovered only when this idea was abandoned.

Herodotus was not the only person in classical times to write about Egypt. Strabo, a Greek geographer and historian born in about 63 B.C., devoted the seventeenth volume of his *Geography* to Egypt and Africa. A far-ranging traveler, Strabo had gone to Egypt with a Roman army in about 25 B.C. and visited as far south as Upper Egypt. Another Greek traveler and geographer, Pausanias, who lived in the second century A.D., wrote about Egypt from firsthand experience. While in Egypt, he saw the pyramids and heard the music of the "singing" Memnon, one of the marvels of ancient times.

This wonder, reported for centuries, has not survived to modern times. The so-called Colossi of Memnon are two gigantic statues of seated figures, found at Thebes, though only the northern of the two statues gave forth a musical tone. Actually, they are statues of Pharaoh Amenhotep III (c. 1412–1380 B.C.), but they were named by early Greek travelers who did not know this. According to all accounts, as soon as the sun's rays touched the statue in the early morning, it seemed to come to life and give forth a sweet and melodious twanging sound.

By the sixteenth century the fanciful misconceptions about Egypt were outweighing the recorded facts. Johannes Helffrich, a German traveler who published an account of Egypt in 1579, helped build the mystery. Four years earlier he had gone to see the pyramids and found nearby "a large head, hewn out of stone, towering on high." This, of course, was the Sphinx, but Helffrich reported, wrongly, that it was hollow. Egyptian priests, he said, climbed into the head and fooled the people into thinking that it spoke.

Helffrich's account of entering the great Pyramid of Cheops is a typical mixture of precise fact and mystery-laden fancy. Identifying it as the tomb of the pharaoh who drowned in the Red Sea, he provides a detailed description of how his party climbed up the passage to the interior. Describing the "musty atmosphere" that greeted them, he goes on to say that the whole group was so affected by the unhealthy air that they became weak the next night and, within two days, "could stir neither arm nor leg."

Knowledge of Egypt was very limited until the end of the eighteenth century. Twelve obelisks in Rome and statues of lions on the steps of the Capitol (now removed) were the principal examples of Egyptian art in Europe. Some scattered statuary in other places, mostly private estates, were generally from the later, Hellenistic, periods, and not true samples of Egyptian culture. The most common Egyptian artifacts in Europe were scarabs, representations of a beetle, used as rings, amulets, or ornaments. The writings of Herodotus and Strabo were known to scholars, but to few others. More recent descriptions usually concerned four topics: the sixty-seven pyramids in the area around Cairo; the Sphinx of Gizeh; obelisks; and the mysterious hieroglyphics that covered nearly every ancient structure.

The long centuries of darkness that had shrouded Egypt came to an abrupt end in 1798, when a French army under General Bonaparte invaded the country. Though Bonaparte's Egyptian campaign was a tragic adventure militarily, its side effects were of lasting importance to science and culture. Egyptology as a science began with French intervention in that ancient land of mystery.

Chapter Two

Frenchmen, Turks, and Mamelukes

I

Twenty years before Bonaparte's invasion a certain Baron de Tott had been sent by the French Foreign Office to inspect French consular and commercial establishments in the Near East. Actually, he was also instructed to explore the possibilities of France's taking over Egypt. This part of his mission was secret because Egypt was under the control of Turkey, and since 1536, under a treaty arranged by Francis I and Suleiman the Magnificent, France and Turkey had been allied.

French interest in Egypt was understandable—Egypt controlled the land routes to Arabia and India. Moreover, as early as 1586 a Turkish engineer had proposed a Suez canal, opening a short sea route to the Orient. But Egypt was also a pawn in France's moves against her traditional enemy, England. Louis XIV had suggested an invasion of Egypt as a move against England's growing power, but nothing was done about it. More important, France had the largest trade with Egypt of any European country and thus had the largest interest there.

The English had established a consulate in Cairo in 1698, but most of the foreign merchants in Egypt were French. These merchants, fifty or sixty of them, lived in walled compounds, called fonduks, in Cairo, Alexandria, Rosetta, and Damietta. They really knew very little about Egypt outside these four cities. But one thing they did know, and report back home, was that the Mamelukes, the local warlords, preferred the British to the French. All in all, French interests demanded an invasion of Egypt.

The 1790's were years of revolution in France. In the early days of the Revolutionary period, France had reason to fear Austria and Russia, as well as England, and no thought could be given to Egypt. But a general named Bonaparte, who would one day be an emperor named Napoleon, fresh from successful campaigns in Italy, cast his eye on Egypt as part of a grand plan of world conquest. In 1797 he wrote to the new foreign minister, Talleyrand, urging that France seize Egypt. Finally, on April 12, 1798, the government ordered the invasion of Malta and Egypt. Though the military considerations were great, there was the added problem of justifying the invasion to Turkey.

Turkish control of Egypt was more nominal than

real. In 1517, Selim I had conquered Egypt and Syria, acquiring for himself and his descendants the title of caliph. Actually, the terms of the conquest were more favorable to the defeated Mamelukes than to the Turks. Each of Egypt's twenty-four provinces was ruled by a Mameluke bey (prince). The twenty-four beys formed a governing council, called a divan, over which the Turkish pasha (governor) presided. By the middle of the eighteenth century, aside from the collection of tribute, called *miry,* the government of Egypt was a farce.

The Mamelukes were the actual lords of the populated portions of Egypt; Bedouin sheikhs controlled the desert. The Turkish pashas, who had nominal and ritual powers, were really puppets of the Mamelukes. Each new pasha was escorted into Cairo by the beys and kept in polite imprisonment during his term of office. Warring beys would force the pashas to issue edicts in their favor. When the French invaded Egypt in 1798, it was the Mamelukes, not the Turks, they had to fight.

II

Egypt in 1798 was at about the lowest point in its long history. Its 2,500,000 population was one-third of what it had been in the days of the pharaohs and one-tenth of what it is today. Nubian tribesmen lived along the Nile in Upper Egypt, and Bedouin tribes roamed the desert, which made up fourteen-fifteenths of the country. The largest part of the population was crowded into the delta, the area at the mouth of the Nile.

The Nile Delta was Egypt's vital center. A pleasant place to live, particularly in winter, it was not too hot and suffered few storms and only rare frosts. Freshwater, distributed through the flat land by numerous canals, was plentiful despite little rain. The air, which was healthfully dry, blew in off the desert, and the atmosphere was muggy only in September, during the Nile floods. The annual flooding of the Nile deposited a rich layer of silt several inches thick throughout the delta. The soil was rich enough to sustain two or three crops every year, chief of which were rice, sugarcane, coffee, tobacco, cotton, flax, lentils, and dates.

There were only two principal cities in Egypt in 1798, both of them in Lower Egypt, the delta region. Alexandria, once second only to Rome, with 4,000 palaces, theaters, temples and monuments, was now a city of 10,000 people living in dust and rubble. Cairo, by comparison, with 250,000 inhabitants, was flourishing—the second most important city in the Near East, after Constantinople. Founded more than 1,000 years earlier and rebuilt many times on the site of an ancient Roman fortress, it was ringed by high walls and dominated by a citadel, built by Saladin in the twelfth century.

Cairo contained large open squares, such as the Ezbekiah, which were flooded and full of boats during the annual inundations of the Nile. From a distance, the domes and minarets of the city's 300 mosques were a striking sight. But close up, Cairo was not so pleasant. Its narrow, dirty, unpaved streets, unlit at night, were

17

flanked by dark houses, falling to pieces. It featured public buildings that looked like dungeons and shops that looked like stables. The prevailing atmosphere was one of dust and garbage.

III

No account of Egypt in 1798 would be complete without a discussion of the Mamelukes. The term means slave or bought man, but the Mamelukes were not slaves in the ordinary sense. They first appeared in Egypt in about 1230. The reigning sultan bought about 12,000 youths, mostly Georgians and Circassians, from the Caucasus Mountains, to form the elite corps of his army. By 1252 they had killed the sultan and taken over Egypt. Their dynasty ruled until the Turkish conquest in 1517, but their power was not diminished by the conquest.

The Mamelukes dominated Egypt for five and a half centuries. They replenished their number, always about 10,000 to 12,000, by buying boys aged eight to ten from the Caucasus and training them as warriors. When a young Mameluke received a military command, he became free. He was then entitled to grow a beard and was given at least two servants-at-arms, called *serradj*. Magnificent horsemen and soldiers whose personal courage was astonishing and proverbial, the Mamelukes were possibly the greatest cavalry fighters of their day.

A Mameluke warrior was a magnificent sight to behold. On his head he wore a green cap wreathed with a large yellow turban. His body was sheathed in a coat of chain mail and a muslin shirt, over which he wore layers of brilliant silk vests and a caftan, a long robe bound at the waist with an embroidered shawl. His legs were covered with gigantic red silk pantaloons, ending in leather gauntlets and red, pointed slippers on his feet. Atop a fine Arab steed, in an enormous saddle of wood and iron, with copper stirrups weighing thirteen pounds, he rode into battle carrying on his person a fortune in jewels, silks, and coins. He was also something of an arsenal on horseback.

"They start like lightning and arrive like thunder," said an observer. Indeed, their fighting style was ferocious. Riding Cossack style, the Mamcluke would fire his carbine and slide it under his thigh, then fire his pistols, throwing them over his shoulder to be picked up by his servants. After this he would throw his javelins and finally charge with his scimitar, sometimes with two scimitars, holding the horse's reins in his teeth. But unhorsed, the Mameluke was too encumbered to fight and had to rely on his Bedouin infantry.

These bloodthirsty warriors were possessed of surprisingly refined taste in their mode of living. Though their houses were rickety structures on the outside, finished in wood or stone, with overhanging balconies, inside they were splendid. Fountains played in marble-lined courtyards, mosaics decorated the walls, and Persian carpets covered the floors. The furniture consisted of little more than divans, but these were richly draped with silk cushions. Each Mameluke maintained a large retinue of slaves. The total number of their dependents was almost ten times the number of warriors.

At the time of the French invasion, the Mamelukes had two leaders. Ibrahim Bey, a tall, thin man in his sixties, with sharp features and an aquiline nose, was Sheikh el-Beled, head of the country. Murad Bey, a plump, bearded man in his forties, was Emir al-Hadj, leader of the annual pilgrimage to Mecca. Their attitude toward the French invaders was simple: The Mamelukes had beaten the French in the twelfth and thirteenth centuries, during the Crusades; they would do so again. Unfortunately for them, the Mamelukes had not changed their mode of warfare since the Crusades, except to replace bows with English carbines, and they assumed the French had changed their fighting methods as little. Not only were they wrong in their assumption, but they neglected something else—the French were commanded by a general named Bonaparte.

Chapter Three

Bonaparte

I

There were four possible routes for an invasion of Egypt in 1798. Two of these, down the Nile from central Africa and across the isthmus of Suez from the east, were not open to the French. A third, across the desert from the west, was not practical. This meant that any invading French army would have to be sailed across the Mediterranean and landed on the flat Egyptian coast at some port city like Alexandria or Rosetta.

Amazingly, such monumental invasion plans remained secret. Long after the French fleet had sailed for Egypt, the British still believed it was headed for Naples or, more likely, through the Strait of Gibraltar for Ireland or England itself. Even the French soldiers, who had been told vaguely that they were to strike a blow against England, were unaware of their destination. One result of this incredible secrecy is that, with the army about to wage war in a country more than nine-tenths desert, no canteens were issued to the soldiers.

THE STONE THAT SPOKE

The invasion plans moved not only secretly but with amazing speed. From government approval of the plan to the actual sailing from Toulon was a matter of ten weeks. In that time Bonaparte had to gather and equip his troops, assemble transports, fit out warships, recruit sailors, and gather a civilian force. The army had about 500 civilians attached to it in administrative capacities, but Bonaparte was also bringing along a Scientific and Artistic Commission. This unique group was to be made up of scientists, engineers, artists, writers, musicians, archaeologists, economists, pharmacists, surgeons, interpreters, and others not usually part of an invading army. Bonaparte's haste in assembling his invasion force was dictated by one central fact. He had to control Egypt before the end of summer and the annual Nile flood.

On May 19, 1798, the French invasion fleet left Toulon. There were 13 ships of the line, carrying 1,026 cannon; 42 frigates, brigs, and smaller vessels; and 130 transports carrying 17,000 troops. In addition, the fleet carried 17,000 sailors and marines, more than 1,000 pieces of field artillery, 100,000 rounds of ammunition, 567 vehicles, 700 horses, and a commanding general, Bonaparte, with quarters aboard the flagship *L'Orient*. This fleet was joined by three smaller convoys to make a total of 400 ships carrying 55,000 men. The combined armada, as it approached the Egyptian coast, covered two to four square miles.

The people ashore were suitably impressed. When they looked at the horizon, said a contemporary observer, the Egyptians "could no longer see water, but only sky and ships: they were seized by unimaginable terror." The invasion was expected, following Bonaparte's seizure of Malta, and the population was in a state of ferment and apprehension. But resistance, dependent on the Mamelukes, was not forthcoming at the moment. The French army landed in darkness and rough seas on the beach at Marabut, a fishing village about eight miles west of Alexandria. On July 1 Bonaparte landed, and the army, seasick, weary, ill-provided, and desperately thirsty, marched on Alexandria. The next morning the city fell after a brief attack.

Murad Bey was in Cairo, assembling an army, of which probably less than half were Mamelukes. The rest were servants-at-arms, Cairo militia, and Bedouins. In order to whip them into a fighting frenzy, Murad warned them about the invaders. "The Infidels who come to fight you," he is reported to have said, "have fingernails one foot long, enormous mouths, and ferocious eyes. They are savages possessed by the Devil, and they go into battle linked together with chains."

Bonaparte sent four divisions, about 18,000 men, south across the desert to battle Murad. At the same time, he dispatched troops to Rosetta, up the coast, and sent his entire fleet to Abukir Bay, situated between Alexandria and Rosetta. Inadequately supplied and virtually without water, the four divisions sought the Mameluke army. Finally, joined by a fifth division and led by Bonaparte, the invaders met the forces of Murad Bey. The contact came at Shubra Khit, on the Nile, more than fifty miles north of Cairo, but no battle ensued.

23

The Mamelukes withdrew, and the French pursued them to Embaba, a village eighteen miles from Cairo, near the great pyramids. There, on July 21, one of the great battles of history took place, and Egypt was suddenly, forcibly, and irreversibly plunged into the modern world.

II

"Soldiers, forty centuries look down upon you." So General Bonaparte addressed his troops before the battle. The pyramids, to which he referred, were actually ten miles away, they were older than forty centuries, and most of the French soldiers had no idea what they were. But the general had a marvelous sense of history, and the name he gave it, the Battle of the Pyramids, is the one by which the massacre of the Mamelukes is known.

The battle itself was simple. The Mamelukes charged the French, drawn up in squares, who held their fire until the last moment. When the smoke cleared, a pile of corpses surrounded each square. The Mamelukes regrouped, charged again, and the massacre continued. Blazing wads from the French muskets hit the Mamelukes along with the bullets, so that the dead and wounded lay with their rich, gauzy uniforms burning fiercely on the desert sands.

After a few charges the Mamelukes fled, many of them drowning in the Nile. Murad Bey fled toward the south, aware that 1,000 or possibly 2,000 of his best men had been killed. Ibrahim Bey, commanding a reserve force on the east bank of the Nile, withdrew to

Cairo and then fled into the Sinai Desert. The battle was over in two hours. Three days later, Bonaparte, a conqueror at the age of twenty-nine, moved into a palace in Cairo. Within a fortnight, however, he and his army were imprisoned in their own conquest. The sudden reversal of Bonaparte's fortune came at sea, in Abukir Bay.

Admiral Nelson, whose sense of history was equal to Bonaparte's, also deliberately misnamed his Egyptian victory. The decisive naval encounter at Abukir has retained the name he gave it—the Battle of the Nile. Nelson had been hunting the French fleet all over the Mediterranean ever since it left Toulon. More than once he had missed it only by odd chance or a trick of fate. But on August 1, French luck ran out.

The French Admiral Brueys had taken his fleet to Abukir on July 7, at Bonaparte's insistence. When Nelson showed up, on the afternoon of August 1, the French were not in a strong position. Almost one-third of the crewmen were on land, looking for provisions. More than half the remaining sailors were inexperienced youths. By 4 o'clock fourteen British ships of the line were bearing down on them to do battle that evening. The first British ships raced into range at sunset, and Brueys had no choice but to fight at anchor.

By 9 P.M. Nelson was incapacitated with a head wound, which he thought to be mortal. His French counterpart, Brueys, was already dead, and the fleets were evenly matched—twelve British battleships to eleven battleships and three frigates on the French side. At 10:15 the tide of battle turned when the French flagship, *L'Orient,* blew up. The flash lit up Alexandria and Rosetta, and the concussion was felt twenty-five miles away. The explosion was followed by ten minutes of complete and eerie silence. Then the fight resumed and continued on and off through the morning of August 2. By 2 P.M. only two French battleships and two frigates were still in condition to fight, but they cut their cables and escaped.

Losses in the battle were enormous. The French lost 1 admiral, 3 captains, and 1,700 men killed in action and 1 admiral, 6 captains, and 1,500 men wounded. The British losses were 218 killed and 677 wounded. Three British ships were dismantled completely and six partially, and two others were temporarily out of action. Nelson left Abukir to have his ships repaired and to bring home his prizes, six French ships. He left a small fleet behind to blockade Egypt and keep Bonaparte's army cut off from the rest of the world.

Despite what seemed a disaster, Bonaparte was not crushed. He proceeded with his plans exactly as if he and his army were not stranded in a hostile foreign land. In fact, the most fascinating, most important, and most consequential phase of the Egyptian campaign was about to get under way. It grew out of the work of the Scientific and Artistic Commission Bonaparte had brought with him to Egypt. Though the French army never succeeded in obtaining a lasting conquest of Egypt, the French civilians did succeed in obtaining a greater conquest. They rescued ancient Egypt from the clutches of time.

Chapter Four

The Institute of Egypt

I

The members of the Scientific and Artistic Commission had been recruited by General François Marie Auguste Caffarelli and the scientist Claude Louis Berthollet. Bonaparte took an active hand in selecting the experts, working through the commission member closest to him, Citizen Monge, whom he had met in Italy. Gaspard Monge, more than twenty years Bonaparte's senior, treated the general like a son. Fifty-two years old in 1798, he had been an associate of the famous chemist Antoine Lavoisier. More recently he had headed the Governmental Commision for the Research of Artistic and Scientific Objects in Conquered Countries. In simple language, this meant that he examined art treasures to be ceded to France. Monge brought many such treasures to France, among them the "Mona Lisa."

The commission consisted of 167 persons, many of them distinguished. The largest contingent was made up of engineers, surveyors, and cartographers, but there were also astronomers, botanists, zoologists, pharmacists, chemists, mineralogists, surgeons, mathematicians, antiquarians (archaeologists), architects, and artists. The chief interpreter was Jean Michel de Venture, a famous Orientalist of that time. Other experts were of equal stature or, like the artist Dominique Vivant Denon, became famous because of their work in Egypt.

Claude Louis Berthollet, the noted physician and chemist, not only helped form the commission, but served as a member. Among his colleagues were Jean Baptiste Joseph Fourier, famous for the Fourier series of equations, and Déodat Guy Silvain Tancrède Gratet de Dolomieu, the mineralogist for whom dolomite is named. Étienne Geoffroy Saint-Hilaire, who taught the first course in zoology in Paris, was another member. Nicolas Jacques Conté, the first military balloonist and the inventor of the graphite pencil, headed the section on mechanics and aerostatics. A mechanical genius, Conté's toolmaking ability proved invaluable throughout the Egyptian expedition.

In the settling-down process that followed the invasion, Bonaparte began to carry out his plans for colonizing Egypt and bringing it into the modern world. One of his early moves was to develop the commission into something more effective than a research team. In an order dated August 22, 1798, he created the Institute of Egypt. Its organization had been worked out by himself, Monge, Berthollet, and a committee of generals and civilians. The members of the institute included the most promising and distinguished members of the Scientific and Artistic Commission, plus various high-ranking officers and administrators.

The first meeting of the institute took place in Cairo on the following day. Monge was elected president, and Bonaparte was elected vice-president. With this formality out of the way, the general immediately proposed six practical problems for consideration by the group. Long-range plans were developed later, and they reflect Bonaparte's ambitious program for a modern, Frenchified Egypt. The institute was created primarily to fulfill practical needs, but it was also intended to provide information, research, and advice. It was divided into four sections: mathematics; physics; political economy; and literature and art. Each section was given or set for itself an enormous study program. Even a partial list of the institute's aims is staggering:

To repair and maintain canals in the delta and plan a canal from the Red Sea to the Mediterranean.

To manufacture articles unobtainable in Egypt.

To reform the fiscal system.

To improve agricultural methods and introduce and experiment with new crops.

To prevent epidemics, reorganize sanitary and hospital services, and particularly to investigate ophthalmia, one of Egypt's most prevalent diseases.

To create an educational system.

To devise a new system of weights and measures.

To study local phenomena, which ranged from mirages to the hippopotamus and the crocodile.

To study the monuments and other antiquities.

To write a history of ancient Egypt.

To prepare a French-Egyptian dictionary.

To preserve freshwater by erecting dams on the Nile.

To examine the causes of the Nile's annual flood.

To observe the sky in the clear Egyptian night.

To carry out a census, map the country, and study its geology and natural history.

The institute also published two journals, and worked for three years to produce the *Description de l'Égypte*. Edmé François Jomard's publication of this work from 1809 to 1813, in ten volumes of text and fourteen volumes of illustrative plates, virtually started the science of Egyptology. Not all the institute's goals were achieved in its time. Some were achieved years later; many of them are being achieved by the present Egyptian government. But the aims of the institute have set the pattern for Egypt's progress ever since 1798.

In time the institute established itself outside Cairo, in the palace of Qassim Bey in the suburb of Nasriya. There, in a complex of buildings, gardens, fountains, and an open-air colonnade, the members studied, labored, and discussed their work. The palace contained a huge garden, which was given over to the botanists, and the busy scientists added a zoological garden, an aviary, a chemical laboratory, a library, an observatory, a museum of natural history, a mineralogical collection, an archaeological collection, and Conté's fabulous workshop.

Gatherings of forty or fifty people took place every evening in the garden of the institute. There the members talked to each other about their discoveries and about Egypt. Soldiers, civilians, generals, and even sheikhs were invited to visit these sessions. There were also regular sessions; the mathematician Fourier, who edited the weekly *Courrier de l'Égypte,* was the permanent secretary to the institute. Questions and practical projects were proposed by Bonaparte, and members pursued projects of their own, everyone meeting every five days to give and receive reports.

II

At the session on July 19, 1799, the members of the institute read a letter from Citizen Lancret announcing "the discovery at Rosetta of some inscriptions that may offer much interest." The discovery had actually been made at Fort Rashid, on the Nile four or five miles northwest of Rosetta. A gang of workmen under the charge of Captain Bouchard had dug up a thick slab of black stone, about the size of a small table, containing three long texts in three different scripts. Though the discovery is credited to a man named Dhautpoul, it was Captain Bouchard who recognized its importance and shipped the stone to Cairo.

When it reached the institute, Citizens Marcel and

Galland made brush proofs of its face, several of which eventually reached Paris. The importance of the slab was also immediately recognized by the institute members. The scholars realized that all three inscriptions were of the same text, but more important, one was in Greek, a language they could translate. It was apparent that the Greek inscription offered a key to the translation of the other two, one of which contained the mysterious hieroglyphics that covered so many of Egypt's relics from the past.

The Rosetta Stone is a slab of fine-grained basalt, 3 feet 9 inches long, 2 feet 4½ inches wide, and 11 inches thick. One of its surfaces is polished, and it is this smooth face that contains the three horizontal columns of writing. The top column consists of fourteen lines of hieroglyphics. Much of this text is missing, and the beginning and end of each line have been lost. The middle column contains thirty-two lines of script which we now know is demotic and which the institute members recognized as being the same as that on many ancient papyruses. Nearly half the lines of this inscription are incomplete. The bottom column contains fifty-four lines of Greek, twenty-six of them mutilated at the ends.

The discovery of this trilingual stone text caused great excitement among the institute members, but it brought them no closer to solving the riddle of hieroglyphics. The promise it held was apparent, but the key to hieroglyphics remained hidden. Moreover, the demotic script presented an added puzzle. We know now that hieroglyphic writing was simplified in ancient Egyptian times to a script called hieratic. After the twenty-fifth dynasty (about 650 B.C.) hieratic was further simplified to a cursive script called demotic. But this knowledge took years of study to acquire.

One thing the institute scholars could determine was the age of the Rosetta Stone. From reading the Greek text they knew that the message, a tribute to Ptolemy V, dated from 196 B.C. This was little information indeed, when it seemed so certain that locked in the mystery of the stone was knowledge of so much greater importance. For the time being, the development of Egyptology rested not at the institute, but with its wandering members in Upper Egypt, particularly with the artist Denon, who was recording the country's wonders in magnificent sketches and drawings. As for the Rosetta Stone, it faced a stormy adventure before revealing its secret.

III

Bonaparte left Egypt late in 1799, slipping past the British blockade at night. He left his second-in-command, General Jean Baptiste Kléber, in charge of the French invasion forces. Kléber was assassinated by a Moslem fanatic on June 14, 1800, and the French command in Egypt fell to the inept General Jacques François de Menou. But the Egyptian campaign was drawing to its ignominious conclusion.

On August 30, 1801, Menou capitulated to a British expeditionary force under General John Hely Hutchinson. The sixteenth article of the capitulation terms declared that all curiosities, natural and artificial, collected by the institute and French individuals were to be delivered to the British. The uproar caused by this edict threatened the whole surrender negotiations. The French scholars, led by Geoffroy Saint-Hilaire, announced that they would follow their collections to England rather than give them up. Menou claimed that the Rosetta Stone was his personal property and the British had no right to it. Numerous letters were exchanged before Hutchinson agreed to a compromise. The natural objects would be considered private property and could remain with the French, but the artificial objects, the antiquities and manuscripts, were to go to the British.

The negotiations were conducted by Major General Sir Tomkyns Hilgrove Turner, whose principal concern was to make sure that the Rosetta Stone became British property. Menou, insisting that it belonged to him, kept it at his house, carefully wrapped in soft cotton cloth and a double matting. There Turner saw it for the first time, increasing his resolve to obtain this treasure above all others.

Eventually Menou gave in, writing to Hutchinson: "You want it, *Monsieur le général?* You can have it, since you are the stronger of us two. . . . You may pick it up whenever you please." Turner arrived with a contingent of soldiers and triumphantly carried off the stone, jeered at by the French as the precious burden was carried through the narrow streets. For a while he kept it in his own quarters, allowing the French scholars to come make casts of its inscribed surface. He personally escorted his prize back to England, arriving at Portsmouth in February, 1802. For a short time, at Turner's request, the stone was kept at the headquarters of the Society of Antiquaries in Deptford. Then it was finally transferred to the British Museum, where it still is, an honored prize of war and a national treasure.

Chapter Five

Puzzling Hieroglyphics

I

When Alexander the Great died, in 323 B.C., his empire was divided among his generals. One of them, Ptolemy, took Egypt for himself and founded his own dynasty. In 58 B.C., in order to keep his throne, one of Ptolemy's descendants called on the Romans to help him. Roman interest continued from that time, and when Cleopatra and her brother fought for the throne, Julius Caesar helped Cleopatra gain control. After Cleopatra's reign, Octavian made Egypt a Roman province. The Greco-Roman period, though covering only a short span in Egypt's long history, had its effect upon the writing of hieroglyphics.

One result of rule by the Ptolemies was the introduction of Greek into Egypt. It became the court language, and all official inscriptions were bilingual. An effort was

even made to express Egyptian speech in Greek characters. To do so, a composite alphabet of thirty-one letters
was needed, with seven being borrowed from the demotic
and hieratic forms of Egyptian writing. During Roman
rule fewer and fewer priests and scribes were trained
to read hieroglyphics. With the coming of Christianity
the temples and schools for scribes were closed, and this
meant the abandonment of hieroglyphics as a living
language.

Near the end of the fourth century A.D., when the
temples were closed, writing in Egypt was done in the
thirty-one-character Greek script. This language was
called Coptic because it was used by the Copts, the
Christian Egyptians. Coptic died out in the sixteenth
century, by which time all Copts spoke Arabic. But the
ancient language of Egypt had died long before. The
last known example of hieroglyphics dates from A.D.
394, and from that time knowledge of hieroglyphics was
lost for 1,400 years.

The first modern study of hieroglyphics dates from
1556 and the publication of G. V. P. Bolzani's *Hiero-
glyphica*. But until the development of Egyptology as a
science in the nineteenth century, most published notions
about hieroglyphics were confused and false. A book
published in 1672, *A Short Collection of the Famous
Mysteries of the Egyptians Named Hieroglyphics,* is little
more than a volume full of nonsense.

The principal source of information, or misinforma-
tion, among early writers on hieroglyphics was Hora-

pollon, who lived in the fourth century A.D. He flatly labeled hieroglyphics picture writing and established the tendency among future scholars to look for symbolic meanings in the pictures. The lists of hieroglyphic signs and their "translations" attributed to Horapollon are largely nothing but nonsense, with occasional true meanings appearing at random.

The most famous of the "decipherers" between ancient and modern times was Athanasius Kircher (1601–1680), who is also credited with having invented the magic lantern. Kircher published four volumes of "translations" between 1650 and 1654, but none of them even remotely fitted the original texts. Kircher had studied Coptic, which he said preserved the language of the ancient Egyptians and, until his death, went on working out his nonsensical translations of hieroglyphics in terms of his Coptic studies.

In 1643, in his book *Lingua Aegyptiaca Restituta,* Kircher called hieroglyphics "this language hitherto unknown in Europe, in which there are as many pictures as letters, as many riddles as sounds, in short as many mazes to be escaped from as mountains to be climbed." This warning from the most famous Egyptologist of his day daunted no one. All through the eighteenth century, scholars pursued the study of hieroglyphics, and travelers made copies of all the inscriptions they could find. So-called translations and theories of all kinds were put forward by insistent but misguided experts. A French student of comparative hieroglyphics announced that the

Chinese were colonists from Egypt, only to be answered by a group of British scholars who said that the Egyptians came from China.

Some theories opened worthwhile leads. Attention was focused on the cartouches, or oval rings, a series of hieroglyphics enclosed in a border. It seemed obvious to some observers that these inscriptions were of special importance, representing in each case either a sacred formula or a royal name. The discovery of the Rosetta Stone promised the first real break in the age-old quest for the key to hieroglyphics, but at first, it only induced even more nonsensical "translations."

The flood of hieroglyphic samples that followed the opening up of Egypt prompted an equal flood of false translations. Various interpreters provided cabalistic, astrological, agricultural, mercantile, and Biblical readings. Someone recognized the Hundredth Psalm in a temple inscription found at Dendera, and the Abbé Tandeau de Saint-Nicolas announced that hieroglyphics was not a system of writing at all, but merely a decorative device.

Study of hieroglyphics now proceeded from two bases, the texts on the Rosetta Stone and the ancient theories of Horapollon. That misleading Greek was presumably an authority; at any rate, he lived closer to the time when hieroglyphic writing was in wide use. Horapollon's chief contribution was the misconception that the hieroglyphics were symbols, conventionalized pictures, which seemed most logical. This notion persisted for centuries, until Young and Champollion abandoned it and found the real key to hieroglyphics.

The Greek text of the Rosetta Stone cleared up some false notions almost at once. A mere reading of the inscription, a praising of Ptolemy V by the priests of Memphis in 196 B.C., pointed out that hieroglyphics was a living language after Herodotus' time and that it was not used exclusively for religious purposes. Moreover, the Greek inscription made clear that all three texts were the same, the other two being in the "writing of the speech of the god" (hieroglyphics) and in the "writing of the books" (demotic). Attempts were made to translate the demotic text, but little more was accomplished than identifying Ptolemy's name. Other names were recognized in time, but the translators were following the old wrong notions. The first scholar to use a different approach was Thomas Young, who saw the demotic inscription as "alphabetic writing" and later achieved some slight success in translating the hieroglyphic portion phonetically.

II

Thomas Young is one of those explorers in the realms of knowledge who stood at the threshold of discovery without crossing over. Born in 1773, this fascinating Englishman was a fluent reader at the age of two. By the time he was twenty, he knew a dozen foreign languages, including Arabic, Persian, and Turkish. In 1798 a legacy from a rich uncle left him financially independent and able to pursue his varied interests, which ranged from the habits of spiders and the theory of tides to hieroglyphics.

He first turned his attention to the Rosetta Stone in 1814, having become intrigued with the problem of hieroglyphics when a friend sent him a papyrus recovered from a Theban mummy case. Because the hieroglyphic portion of the Rosetta Stone was obviously incomplete and he was not sure how much of the text was missing, Young concentrated on the demotic text. His method of attack was to compare words that were repeated within each inscription. For instance, the word "king" appeared in the Greek text thirty-seven times; this undoubtedly had to be matched by a group of demotic characters repeated about thirty times. The name Ptolemy appeared eleven times in the Greek, suggesting that it was the same as a demotic grouping that occurred fourteen times in two variations.

Working in this way, Young compiled a Greek-demotic vocabulary of eighty-six groupings, most of which proved correct. When he attempted a translation of the whole demotic text, however, his effort was mostly guesswork. What he did not know was that the demotic version was only a paraphrase of the Greek, the original text of the message. The hieroglyphic text was also only a paraphrase of the Greek. The fact that the repeated words and names occurred a different number of times in each version should have suggested this to him. It

41

was only in 1850 that demotic became truly understood. and the first accurate and full translation of the demotic portion of the Rosetta Stone was accomplished in 1880.

Having offered what he felt was a translation of the demotic portion, Young turned to the Rosetta Stone's hieroglyphic text. Here his ingenuity served him better, for he actually hit on the first major breakthrough in the translation of hieroglyphics. If the Egyptian scribes had to write the unfamiliar names of non-Egyptians, their foreign conquerors, reasoned Young, they would have to resort to phonetic values to transcribe these names. Moreover, if the cartouches that had attracted so much scholarly attention were indeed names of kings, then the name Ptolemy could be picked out, and phonetic values could be assigned to its elements.

Young decided that he had found "Ptolemy" in the sixth line, in the cartouche

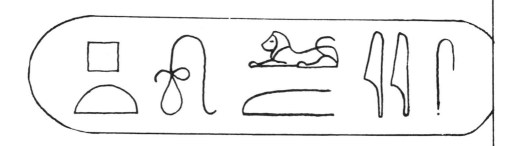

which is transcribed here left to right for convenience.

A longer version appeared in the fourteenth line, but the demotic text also had different versions of the name that Young was convinced was Ptolemy's. This variation did not trouble Young because the Greek text indicated that the longer version of a name simply included a title along with the name. It was the same as saying "Elizabeth" and "Queen Elizabeth" in an English proclamation.

Equating the hieroglyphic symbols with the elements of Ptolemy's name in Greek, which was Ptolemaios, Young translated the cartouche as

Unfortunately, his translation was partly wrong. Young had forgotten that the Egyptians, following the Semitic practice, usually dropped the vowels from their written words. Actually, some of the signs in the cartouche were vowels, which entered hieroglyphic writing in its later development, but Young designated them incorrectly. His mistake in assigning the vowels eventually threw him off enough to discourage him from working out an accurate translation of hieroglyphics.

43

We know now that the translation should read

but this does not diminish Young's accomplishment. He recognized Ptolemy's name, and he confirmed that the cartouche did contain a royal name. Above all, he introduced the concept of phonetic translation, ending centuries of misguided effort. He outlined his discoveries in an article in the 1819 edition of the *Encyclopaedia Britannica*. In this article he also set down other ingenious discoveries, among them that hieroglyphics should be read in whichever direction the characters faced, that numerals were written as strokes, and how plurals were formed.

The actual discovery of the key to hieroglyphics was made by the Frenchman Champollion, but how much credit should go to Thomas Young, the discoverer on the threshold? Young gained a limited success in deciphering demotic, working phonetically. He revised his theory when working on hieroglyphics, dividing them into letters, monosyllables, and disyllables. He was an

44

ingenious interpolator, but basic problems escaped his grasp, perhaps because he was not a philologist, a true scholar of language itself. Champollion, who was a philologist and a master of more than a dozen ancient languages, was better equipped in the basics of linguistics. Young could guess correctly at the meanings of words; Champollion could recognize the linguistic system underlying the words.

When he abandoned his study of hieroglyphics, Young said his system would lead to the decipherment of that ancient language. But in giving up his studies, he seemed to indicate his own bafflement. He was content to translate some words and royal names. For Champollion, this was only the starting point. His is the greater glory because his was the greater vision. That vision included recognizing the importance of another object dug out of the Egyptian sands—the Obelisk of Philae.

Chapter Six

Champollion Finds the Key

I

His birth was predicted by a magician and his genius was hailed by an emperor. His colleagues alternately honored him and hounded him as a traitor. Without having seen it, he knew more about Egypt than people who had been there. He struggled for recognition throughout his life but is remembered as the greatest of all linguistic decipherers. He is Jean François Champollion, discoverer of the key to hieroglyphics.

Champollion was born in Figeac, a little town in southeastern France, on December 23, 1790. Though his father was a simple librarian and bookseller, Champollion seems to have been a rare and unusual person. His mother had been sick and was cured by a "magician" who said she would give birth to a boy who would become famous and remembered for centuries. The first unusual thing anyone noticed about him was his seemingly Oriental appearance. Even in later life, because of his features and coloring, he was known as the Egyptian.

More striking qualities became evident as he grew up. He was a noticeably bright boy, teaching himself how to read at the age of five. His brother Jacques Joseph, who was twelve years older and himself a scholar, took young Jean's education in hand. This brotherly devotion continued throughout Champollion's life, and Jacques Joseph even called himself Champollion-Figeac so as not to detract from his younger brother's glory.

When he was eleven, Champollion, already fluent in Latin and Greek, began studying Hebrew. He was introduced to Fourier, who was impressed enough with the boy to show him his collection of antiquities brought back from his Egyptian adventure with Bonaparte. When told by Fourier that no one could read hieroglyphics, Champollion is supposed to have replied, "I am going to do it." In a few years, he told the famous mathematician, when he was bigger, he would be able to read the puzzling symbols. At thirteen he was moving toward his goal, learning Arabic, Syriac, Chaldean, and Coptic.

At seventeen, a student at the university at Grenoble, he drew up a chart outlining the history of ancient Egypt. He wanted to transfer from Grenoble to the *lycée* in Paris, and to obtain entrance there, he wrote a book, *Egypt Under the Pharaohs*. But when the staff at Grenoble heard him read the introduction to his book, he was promptly made a member of the faculty. The president of the Grenoble Academy enthusiastically proclaimed: "In appointing you a member despite your youth, the Academy has taken into account the work you have already done, but looks forward to what you will achieve in the future. We like to think that you will justify our hopes, that one day your works will make a name for you and that you will recall that you received your first encouragement from this Academy." Paris, however, was a better place to pursue Champollion's study of Oriental languages, and he felt compelled to go there. He was forced to live in the great city in the utmost poverty, supported only by his brother's generosity. It was there that he first studied the Rosetta Stone, or rather a newly made copy sent over from London. At that time Champollion did not attempt to decipher the stone; he simply compared it with a papyrus in his possession.

During his stay in Paris, Champollion underwent a most unnerving experience. One day he was shocked to learn that another scholar, a friend named Alexandre Lenoir, had announced that he had deciphered the mysterious hieroglyphics. In a frenzy, Champollion rushed out to buy Lenoir's book, *Nouvelle Explication*. Back in his room, he raced through the book, recognizing immediately that Lenoir's efforts were sheer nonsense. Champollion was so relieved to find this out that he rocked uncontrollably in hysterical laughter. But his sense of shock and his violent reaction reinforced his boyhood vow that *he* would be the person who finally deciphered hieroglyphics.

In July, 1809, not quite nineteen, he was back at Grenoble as a professor of history. As any such prodigy might, he incurred the enmity of jealous older professors, though he was unaware of doing so. He went about his teaching and his studies, paying little attention to events around him. But events were about to catch up with the unwitting scholar. These were the closing years of Napoleon's reign, and the emperor, who as General Bonaparte had opened Egypt to the Western world, was about to influence the life of the man who rescued Egypt from the shrouds of time.

In 1815, when Napoleon returned from his temporary exile at Elba, he passed through Grenoble. There he met Champollion and had two long discussions with the young scholar. The two men may have been introduced by Champollion's brother, who had become one of Napoleon's secretaries. When royalist armies marched on Grenoble, Champollion helped man the walls in the city's defense. As soon as the firing started, however, alone and at the risk of his life, Champollion rushed back to the university library to put out fires caused by the bombardment and thus save his precious papyruses. After Napoleon's final defeat, because of his connection with the emperor, Champollion was banned from the university for more than a year by his jealous older colleagues.

The shadow of Napoleon stretched out to influence

Champollion again in July, 1821. The threat of renewed treason charges caused him to flee Grenoble for Paris. There he continued his work of deciphering hieroglyphics and, in 1822, published his famous *Lettre à M. Dacier relative à l'alphabet des hiéroglyphes phonétiques* (Letter to Mr. Dacier Concerning the Alphabet of the Phonetic Hieroglyphics). This work outlined the basic principles of the first successful method for deciphering the age-old language of mystery.

II

How much Champollion owed to Young is open to question. As late as 1821 he wrote that the hieroglyphics were representative of things, not sounds. Sometime in that year he could have seen Young's *Encyclopaedia Britannica* article, though he said he did not. However, he was, like Young, familiar with the Ptolemy cartouche. But here is the important point. As Young's incorrect translation indicates, more than one royal name was necessary to prove the correctness of the phonetic theory. The second name, the code breaker, was supplied by the Philae Obelisk.

Almost from the day of its discovery the Rosetta Stone had been looked upon as the key to unlocking the hieroglyphic puzzle. Yet more than twenty years of scholarly endeavor had accomplished little in the way of decipherment. The Philae Obelisk, from the time of its discovery in 1815 by the Englishman W. J. Bankes, was regarded as a second Rosetta Stone. But it too remained tantalizingly indecipherable. A royal decree, inscribed in about 190 B.C. in hieroglyphics and Greek, it contained the royal names Ptolemy and Cleopatra. This much was known from the Greek text, and the hieroglyphic text contained a cartouche that matched the Ptolemy cartouche on the Rosetta Stone. Presumably, then, a second cartouche on the Philae Obelisk had to represent Cleopatra's name. All this seemed clear to Champollion, to whom a copy of the Philae Obelisk was sent in January, 1822.

Certain other points were clear to Champollion. In their Greek form, the names of Ptolemy and Cleopatra had several letters in common. They also contained letters that were different. The comparison of similar and dissimilar elements suggested a phonetic approach. "The interpretation of the *demotic* text on the Rosetta inscription, by means of the accompanying Greek text," wrote Champollion, "had made me realize that the Egyptians used a certain number of *demotic* characters, which assumed the property of expressing sounds, to introduce into their ideographic writings *proper names* and *words foreign to the Egyptian language.*"

Standing on the threshold abandoned by Young, Champollion moved forward to achieve success and the everlasting glory that had been predicted for him. He made a tentative comparison of the two royal cartouches. Three of the signs in Ptolemy's cartouche, those for *P, O,* and *L,* corresponded to signs in Cleo-

51

patra's. Moreover, two similar signs in Cleopatra's cartouche corresponded to the position of the *A* in her name. However, the *T* signs in the two cartouches were different, but Champollion correctly regarded them as homophones. The comparison worked out this way

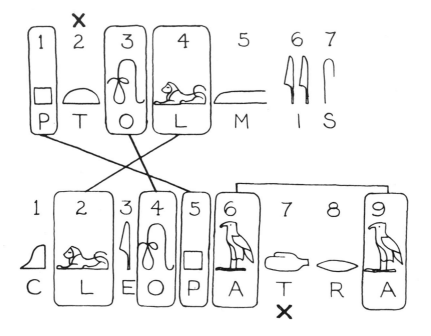

With this initial effort, Champollion confirmed the phonetic nature of hieroglyphics. The two names, he wrote, "which have certain like letters in Greek, had to

serve for a comparative study of the hieroglyphic symbols which composed the two; and if identical signs in these two names stood for *the same sounds* in both cartouches, they would have to be *entirely phonetic* in character." Moreover, he could now designate values for a dozen hieroglyphic signs. To confirm his discovery, he proceeded to apply the symbols he "knew" to another cartouche. (Again, the hieroglyphics are arranged left to right for convenience.)

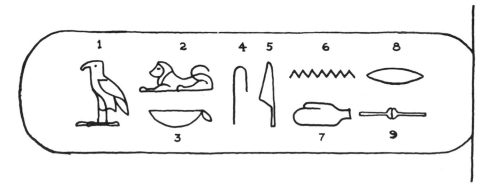

He already knew symbols 1, 2, 4, 5, 7 and 8, which gave him the following:

```
1 2 3 4 5 6 7 8 9
A L   S E   T R
```

Only one name, Alksentrs, the Greek for Alexander, fitted this combination, so 3 more signs were added to his alphabet. Working in this way with the names of rulers and their titles, Champollion built an alphabet of 80 signs within a few weeks and soon enlarged it to 100. But all these signs were worked out from cartouches of the Greco-Roman period in Egypt's long history. What about the language of pre-Alexandrine times? Young had felt that phonetic hieroglyphics was a Greek innovation. Was this so?

"I am positive," wrote Champollion, "that the same signs in *phonetic hieroglyphics* used to represent the sounds of Greek and Roman proper names were also used in ideographic texts carved long before the Greeks reached Egypt, and that they already had, in certain contexts, the same value representing sounds or articulations as in the cartouches carved under the Greeks and Romans. . . . I believe that *phonetic* writing existed in Egypt at a far distant time; that it was first a necessary part of the ideographic script and that it was then used also . . . to transcribe (crudely, it is true) in ideographic texts the proper names of peoples, countries, cities, rulers and individual foreigners who had to be commemorated in historic texts or monumental inscriptions." At the time he wrote this, Champollion considered a demonstration of the proof of his statement too long and complicated to go into. On September 14, 1822, he began working on an inscription from an obviously ancient temple.

III

When Champollion began work on the ancient inscription, he had already reached some further helpful conclusions. For one thing, he had recognized the existence of determinatives—silent signs at the end of words, placed there to give more accurate definition to words that were written the same but were phonetically different, a situation arising from the absence of written vowels. Moreover, he had determined why certain signs or symbols were used. Once the represented object could be identified, wrote Champollion, "it would be a relatively easy matter for me to show . . . that the names of these same objects begin with the consonant or vowels which their image represents in the phonetic hieroglyphic system." In other words, using English examples, a picture of a man would represent the *m* sound, or that of a dog would represent the *d* sound. One other helpful conclusion reached by Champollion concerned the relation of hieroglyphics to demotic. "There is," he wrote, "basically no other difference between the *hieroglyphic* and *demotic* alphabets but the actual form of the signs, their values and even the reasons for those values being identical."

Armed with his remarkable understanding of basic principles, Champollion could proceed with the decipherment of his ancient inscription. His first step was to find recognizable signs in the inscription. Once again, he turned to the cartouches.

55

In one of them he found a double *s* preceded by two unknown signs. The first of these unknown signs was an emblem of the sun. In Coptic, he knew, the word for sun was Ra or Re, but the middle symbol remained unknown. However, the formation Ra plus unknown plus *ss* suggested to him a familiar name, that of the Pharaoh Rameses. Checking back with the Rosetta Stone, he associated the unknown middle sign with the Greek word for birthday. Drawing again on his knowledge of Coptic, he recalled that "be born" was *ms* and "child" was *mas*. Both these words related to "birthday." The identification with the name Rameses seemed proved; moreover, the pharaoh's name could be interpreted as "child of Ra," which was a logical meaning.

A second cartouche confirmed his opinion. This one contained three signs, the first unknown but the other two representing *mes*. The unknown first sign was the figure of an ibis, a large Nile bird related to the heron. The ibis was also the symbol of the god Thoth. So he could read this name as Thothmes or Thotmss. It suggested another name of a familiar pharaoh, Thutmose. And the pharaoh's name could be taken to mean "child of Thoth."

This monumental feat of decipherment revealed a fascinating proposition. Hieroglyphics was not just phonetic, nor was it, as had been believed, symbolic. It was a combination of both. As Champollion put it, in his *Précis du système hiéroglyphique* (1824), the ancient

56

writing was "figurative, symbolical, and phonetic in the same text, in the same phrase, in the same word." The mystery more than 1,000 years old had been solved. The way was open for a century of scholars to step in and continue the work of translating the countless inscriptions that covered the monuments of ancient Egypt.

IV

Champollion accomplished his great feat of decipherment and built up his extensive knowledge of the ancient kingdom without having set foot in Egypt. At last, in July, 1828, he visited the country that had occupied so much of his thoughts and efforts. For a year and a half, until December, 1829, he toured the various sites he had studied from afar and confirmed theories he had propounded from his scholar's desk. His tour, sponsored by the admiring French government, was a triumph.

The personal triumph and the scholarly satisfaction Champollion felt seem to have been mixed with a joyous holiday feeling. He dressed in the costume of the country and, by all accounts, looked and acted exactly like a native. One night, he and his party of fifteen colleagues visited the temple at Dendera. They left their boat, slipped past palm trees and through tall grass, and crashed through thorns and bushes for more than two hours. At one point they called out into the night and were answered by the distant barking of a dog; at another they picked up a frightened native. Singing songs, they trudged on until, at last, they came to the temple, silent and bathed in moonlight.

It was the first large, well-preserved Egyptian temple Champollion had ever seen. "I will not try to describe," he wrote, "the impression that the temple, and in particular its portico, made on us. The separate dimensions of the structure can be measured, but it is quite impossible to give an idea of the whole. To the highest imaginable degree the temple combines grace with majesty. We stayed there two hours, filled with ecstacy. Guided by our poor wretch of a fellah, we wandered through the halls and tried to read the inscriptions on the outside in the glittering moonlight."

His brilliant mind could never content itself with simple appreciation. The temple had been regarded as one devoted to Isis, but Champollion identified it as being a temple of Hathor, the goddess of love. Proclaiming it "an architectural masterpiece," he noted that it was overlaid "with sculpture in the worst style." His keen eye had recognized at once that the original structure was marred by later additions. It was a moment of exaltation, and the whole trip was enjoyed to the fullest. Three years later, Champollion was dead.

From 1824 until his death, Champollion worked continuously at the study of hieroglyphics. In addition to visiting Egypt, he traveled throughout Europe examining collections of papyruses. He gathered an enormous amount of material but died before he had arranged it all. His brother, devoted as ever, took over his work and published his Egyptian grammar and dictionary posthumously. Though he had many other champions and friends, Champollion's work was not accepted by everyone. When the German Egyptologist Karl Richard Lepsius supported his theories, in 1837, they were still controversial. In 1866, Lepsius and other German scholars, working on a newly discovered bilingual text, confirmed Champollion's pioneering efforts. By this time hieroglyphic writing was studied in a truly scientific manner, and Champollion's contributions could not be denied. Official recognition came sixty-four years after his death, when the Royal Society of London honored Champollion for his work in deciphering hieroglyphics. That was in 1896, ninety-five years after the boy of eleven had said, "I am going to do it."

Chapter Seven

Pictures, Sounds, and Words

I

Hieroglyphics (the name applies to both the language and the symbols) was rescued from 1,400 years of oblivion; it had been a living language for more than twice that length of time. Over the years, its use became less generalized, more specialized, and was restricted to priests and their scribes. The associated cursive script is known as hieratic, a name derived from the Greek word for priestly.

Examples of hieratic writing indicate that its use dates back to very ancient times. It came into being with the use of papyrus and the development of the reed pen. The angular shapes of the carved hieroglyphic characters became rounded when written with a pen. After a while some pictorial forms were no longer recognizable in their hieratic version. Also, writing settled into a horizontal, rather than a vertical, form. Eventually another script, demotic, which was even more abbreviated, evolved from the hieratic writing.

By Roman times there were three definite styles of writing in Egypt: hieroglyphic, for sacred inscriptions on temples and monuments; hieratic, for priestly purposes; and demotic, for daily use. Roughly speaking, these three forms corresponded to printing, handwriting, and shorthand. In post-Roman times, still another form, Coptic, developed.

As would be expected in anything that lasted for more than 4,000 years, the Egyptian language underwent several changes. These stages of linguistic development have been classified as Old Egyptian, Middle Egyptian, Late Egyptian, Demotic, and Coptic. Old Egyptian grew into Middle Egyptian toward the end of the ninth dynasty, about 2100 B.C. or earlier. Used for literary purposes down to Greco-Roman times, Middle Egyptian was the language of the classic age of Egyptian writing. Late Egyptian was the vernacular of the eighteenth through twenty-fourth dynasty, a period of about eight centuries starting in 1567 B.C. Demotic was the script used in documents dating from the twenty-fifth dynasty on, and the use of Coptic dates from the third century A.D.

There are more than 700 known hieroglyphs—that is, symbols that have been identified and for which meanings have been assigned. Many of them represent parts of humans and animals; 54 are representations of birds. Recognition of what these symbols pictured, as well as

61

what they meant, came gradually. Thomas Young, in his pioneering efforts, referred to "a Square, a Semicircle, a figure often called Feathers, and a vertical line not unlike a Crook." We now know that these are representations of a stool, a loaf, a flowering reed, and a folded cloth.

Hieroglyphic writing was invariably arranged with an eye for its decorative effect. The symbols may appear in vertical columns or horizontal lines. They are usually read from the right to the left, but not always. Signs that can be said to have a face almost always face the beginning of the inscription, indicating the direction in which it is to be read. Sometimes, in keeping with the decorative effect, symbols appear one on top of another within a horizontal inscription. Symbols on top take precedence over those under them. Each group of hieroglyphs is usually symmetrically arranged to fit within an invisible rectangle. As much as their architecture or painting, their writing indicates how much the ancient Egyptians were conscious of beauty.

II

There are two main groups of hieroglyphics—ideograms and phonograms. An ideogram, or word-sign, indicates the object it depicts, though it can, in some cases, also stand for an associated idea. The double use of ideograms is not peculiar to hieroglyphics. In any picture writing it is reasonable to assume that a symbol representing the sun may mean sun and also day. A phonogram, or sound-sign, is an ideogram that has taken on a phonetic value and is used for a word that cannot be drawn as a sign or symbol. In hieroglyphic writing, one or more phonograms might be followed by an ideogram indicating the general meaning of the signs preceding it.

Though scholars can read hieroglyphics and know that some of the symbols are phonograms, they cannot pronounce the language—more specifically, their attempts at pronunciation arc only guesswork at best. It is difficult to reconstruct the sound of a language that is written without vowels. The word *htp* is presumably *hotep*, or so we now believe; but it is also felt that some combinations, depending on the context in which they are placed, can be rendered in various ways. Thus, the combination *nfr* can be worked out as *nafre* or *nofra* or *nofre* or even *nofri*, each of which is a different word. We know that the Egyptian scribes not only omitted many vowels when they wrote, but also dropped most short words and all punctuation. It was as if you were to write "Grl pt pn dn" for the sentence "The girl put the pen down." Even someone familiar with your abbreviated method of writing could not be certain whether the girl put down a pen, a pan, or a pin. Translating hieroglyphics is far from simple, and the language has its own built-in booby traps.

Not only Champollion and Young, but all the early translators were drawn to the cartouches. These sets of hieroglyphs contained within oval lines, with a stroke at the beginning, occur at intervals in practically all the Egyptian inscriptions. The early supposition that they contained the names of kings and queens proved substantially correct. The term "cartouche" comes from the French word for cartridge, which is what this configuration looked like to Bonaparte's soldiers. Actually, it represents a rope tied with a knot. Why this device was employed is not known for certain. Perhaps it symbolized the fact that the pharaoh owned everything that the sun went around.

When translation of the hieroglyphic inscriptions began on a scientific basis, religious messages, as expected, were the ones most frequently deciphered. But, it soon developed, hieroglyphics had not been used exclusively for religious purposes. Scholars began to translate inscriptions that turned out to be historical and official documents. They also discovered medical and mathematical treatises. A certain amount of general literature also turned up, and today, thousands of years later, Egyptian stories, fables, poems, and hymns survive for the scholars to read.

So far no major works of literature have been found, and it is believed that ancient Egypt produced none. One other lack is even more noticeable. Despite all the advances and changes in their language over many centuries, the Egyptians never developed a purely alphabetic script. Any reference to a hieroglyphic "alphabet" is a matter of convenience; the Egyptians themselves never comprehended the convenience a true alphabet provides.

III

Hieroglyphics probably began as picture writing pure and simple. To express difficult ideas, the Egyptians most likely devised a kind of rebus. The rebus survives today in popular puzzles, the kind in which a picture of a bee and a picture of a leaf are put together to make the word "belief." But this outline of the development of hieroglyphics is only guesswork. The oldest known hieroglyphs date from 3100 B.C., and they are examples of a fully developed written language.

Though the Egyptians had no alphabet as such, they did have a symbol for every consonant sound in their speech. This arrangement was efficient enough for them, and they made no attempt to symbolize vowels except in the phonetic reproduction of foreign names. Combinations of phonograms could be used to form the basic version of any word the Egyptian scribe was required to set down. What served for an "alphabet" consisted of more than 100 representations of consonantal sounds. There were 24 single-consonant sounds, also known as unilaterals or uniconsonantal signs, plus 75 bilaterals and a number of trilaterals, or multiconsonantal signs. A look at some of them indicates why hieroglyphics, even when untranslated, is so visually fascinating.

UNILITERALS

(SOUND)
m
(OWL)

n
(WATER)

r
(MOUTH)

t
(LOAF)

s
(BOLT)

(TWISTED
FLAX)

BILITERALS

hr
(FACE)

me
(MILK JUG
IN A NET)

wr
(BIRD)
(SWALLOW
OR MARTIN)

TRILITERALS

kheper
(BEETLE)
(OR SCARAB)

ankh
(SANDAL
STRAP)

Both the efficiency and the shortcomings of the Egyptian system can be seen in the example of a word, "crocodile," common enough in the usage of someone who lived on the Nile. To write the word for crocodile, the Egyptian scribe used three consonants, *m, s,* and *h,* which he set down as an owl, a bolt, and twisted flax.

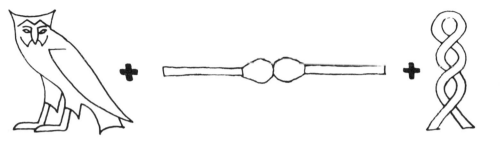

This may have been pronounced *meseh* or *miseh,* if we add the probable vowels, but it also may have been pronounced *emseh.* A picture of a crocodile may have been added by the scribe, as a purely visual symbol, just for emphasis. The scribes often added signs for emphasis, and not necessarily visual ones. Phonetic complements were also added to assist the reader; for example:

in which the *wr* sign is followed by the *r* sign for phonetic emphasis.

Of about 700 hieroglyphs in use in the New Kingdom (1567–1085 B.C.), at least 100 were purely visual. Sometimes these symbols were used simply to represent the desired word; often they were added to the phonetic representations to provide the reader with an aid or guide. The word *tekhen,* meaning "obelisk," was written phonetically as *t* plus *kh* plus *n* and was generally followed by a symbol of an obelisk. These visual signs had to be readily identifiable. That the following

meant weep, beer pot, man, and hill country or desert is not too hard to imagine. Because so many words could be read as homonyms or near homonyms (as in the English words "wait," "weight," and "wade"), the scribes were liberal in their use of determinative symbols to help the reader grasp the correct meaning.

The use and importance of determinatives is demonstrated by the case of *hnw*. Written as follows,

the word could be pronounced *hinew* or *ohanow* or several other ways and could have a number of meanings, among them liquid measure, rejoicing, and neighbors. Such a protean word had to appear with a determinative to be properly understood. Thus

 *h* plus *n* plus *w* plus determinative,

in which the determinative is a beer pot, the meaning is liquid measure. If the determinative were a sign showing a man and a woman over three parallel strokes (the way in which plural was symbolized), then the meaning would have to be neighbors. In this way, with the use of different determinatives, one grouping of letters could indicate as many as ten different words.

IV

The once-mysterious hieroglyphic inscriptions that cover the monuments and fill the papyruses of ancient Egypt have increased in fascination with the solving of their mystery. In them is contained the story of every aspect of life in ancient Egypt. The scholarly treasure they held, or withheld, was scarcely imagined by the earliest explorers.

Auguste Mariette, the founder of the Egyptian Museum, was well aware of the significance of Champollion's accomplishment. In 1877 he wrote: "The amount of information already obtained from the deciphering of hieroglyphics, though this science is still in its infancy, is already immense. What will it be when several generations of savants shall have studied those admirable ruins, of which one may truly say that the more they are known, the more they repay the labor bestowed upon them?" The years since 1877 have provided admirable answers to this question.

One of the major benefits derived from an understanding of hieroglyphics was the development of an Egyptian chronology. Many inscriptions contained lists of kings, divided into dynasties. When these were added together and checked for accuracy a reasonable time-table of reigns could be devised. Other inscriptions contained astronomical data about the movements of stars, which archaeologists checked with astronomers and mathematicians. By cross-checking the royal lists and the astronomical information and fixing dates with scientific accuracy, a reliable chronology could be devised. Despite the advances of science, Egyptian chronology still clings to one nonscientific pattern. Shortly after the death of Alexander the Great, about 300 B.C., a priest named Manetho of Sebennytus wrote a history of Egypt. This fanciful account, written in Greek, is known to be inaccurate in recording the lengths of various reigns. But it is Manetho's list of pharaohs, divided into thirty dynasties, that is still in use.

The Rosetta Stone is the most famous of the inscribed tablets to have emerged from ancient Egypt, but it is not the only useful one. Champollion could not have achieved his success without the Philae Obelisk. The chronologists have relied on other steles. Their names alone capture the imagination—the Royal Tablet of Karnak, the Royal Tablet of Sakkara, the Royal List of Abydos. One of the more fascinating relics is the Palermo Stone, only a fragment, but considered to be the oldest record we have from ancient Egypt.

The story of Egypt is written in its stones. On countless temple walls, on myriad obelisks, at the base of the Sphinx and numerous monumental statues, heiroglyphics appear. Mariette, once again, has summarized their significance in a few sentences. "There is no need," he wrote, "to enlarge upon the importance of the monuments that cover the banks of the Nile. They are the witnesses of Egypt's former greatness, and, so to speak, the patents of her ancient nobility. They represent in the eyes of strangers the tattered pages of the archives of one of the most glorious nations in the world."

Chapter Eight

Land Between the Rivers

I

If Egypt was, as Herodotus said, the "gift of the river Nile," then Mesopotamia was the gift of two rivers, the Tigris and the Euphrates. Rising amid the everlasting snows of the mountains of Armenia, more than 13,000 feet high, they flow their parallel but separate ways down to the Persian Gulf. Today they have a common mouth, but in ancient times, when the coastline extended much farther north, this was not so. Over the centuries silt deposits formed a delta, and cities that were once coastal came to lie farther and farther inland. In time their ruins were covered by desert sands. But in ancient times, in order to prevent spring floods in the land between the rivers, canals were built to divert and distribute the annual floodwaters.

Beyond the region of canals lay an ageless swamp, filled with shallow waters, huge reeds, and scattered tiny islands. The two main areas of ancient Mesopotamia, roughly that of modern Iraq, were startlingly different. The swamp and fertile plain of the south gave way to desert and high mountains. From the earliest times, differences in climate, topography, products, resources, and ways of life between the northern and southern areas have been noted. The mountains of the north are rich in minerals, and ancient records tell of a downriver commerce bringing iron, copper, precious metals, naphtha, and bitumin from Assyria to Babylonia, which had none of these resources.

Mesopotamia lies at a crossroads of land and water routes from every direction. Though its communication routes from north and east are over mountains, these were the routes taken by its eventual conquerors. The long history of Mesopotamia is one of successive conquests by invaders interspersed with revolts and returns to power of the defeated. The principal builders of Mesopotamian civilization were two peoples of different origin, the Sumerians and the Akkadians. They lived in so intermingled a fashion that Mesopotamian history and culture are the result of a synthesis in which it is often impossible to distinguish the Sumerian from the Akkadian.

Today our knowledge of Mesopotamia is full enough to eliminate the confusions of the past. We can understand things that were unclear to the nineteenth-century scholars, and we possess information unknown or unavailable to the Biblical writers and such classical historians as Herodotus. Armed with this knowledge, we can ap-

proach ancient Mesopotamia considerably better informed than the scholars and excavators who brought it
to light after centuries of burial in the dust.

II

The people who lived in ancient Mesopotamia were of
the group we call Semitic, though we know now that
they were not the original settlers. The name Semitic
comes from the Bible. The book of Genesis names the
sons of Noah, one of whom was Shem, and his sons were
Aram, Asshur, and Eber. From them we derive the names
of three Shemitic, or Semitic, peoples: the Aramaeans,
the Assyrians, and the Hebrews. Archaeology has brought
to light other peoples with similar characteristics. The
common characteristics that distinguish the Semitic peoples are mainly linguistic, but they are also bound by
geography and a common historical and cultural tradition.

The Sumerians, who preceded the Semites, were most
likely established in southern Mesopotamia in prehistoric
times. They attained a high level of civilization very early
and were certainly one of the oldest cultures in the world.
The Sumerians dug canals, farmed, built temples, and
carved statues; in short, they established a true civilization, which was organized into city-states with priest-
kings. Continual rivalry among the cities, with the brief
rise to power of one city or another, kept them from
establishing a strong nation. The only notable Sumerian

ruler was Lugalzaggisi, a King of Umma, which was conquered in about 2350 B.C. by a Semitic dynasty.

Semitic groups had been in Mesopotamia long before
the victory over Lugalzaggisi, probably for centuries, living on the outskirts of the Sumerian cities. The first great
Semitic king was Sargon, the founder of the Akkadian
dynasty and the semilegendary ruler of Babylonia, Assyria, and Syria. He established a Babylonian state that
survived for several centuries until Babylonia was invaded by a people called Gutians; this allowed a brief
Sumerian revival to take place. About 2000 B.C. a new
Semitic invasion, under the Amorites, established new
cities of power and an Amorite dynasty that remained
preeminent in the area from about 1830 to 1530 B.C.
The sixth king of this dynasty was the famous Hammurabi, whose reign marked a period of great prosperity.

This first Babylonian dynasty fell before a Hittite invasion, which was followed by an invasion from the east
by the Cassites. These invaders, who included some Indo-
European peoples, remained in power until about 1160
B.C. But another Semitic nation, that of the Assyrians,
was rising in northern Mesopotamia. Assyria was a military nation with a highly organized army that had existed
for centuries, growing in power fitfully. By the time of
Tukulti-Ninurta I (1243–1207 B.C.) it had conquered
its neighbors and laid waste to Babylon. A century later,
under Tiglath-pileser I, Assyria's New Empire extended
from the Black Sea to the Mediterranean and eastward
to Babylon.

After being checked for a time, Assyria was restored to prominence under Ashurnasirpal II and reached its height under Tiglath-pileser III, who ruled until 727 B.C. A later king, Sargon II, even conquered Egypt. The last great ruler of Assyria was Ashurbanipal (668–626 B.C.), who is better known by his Greek name, Sardanapalus. In 612 B.C. the Medes, sweeping down from the Iranian plateau, captured the Assyrian capital, the famous city of Nineveh. The Assyrian empire, its palaces, its magnificent library, and its fantastic sculptures were swallowed up by the sands of the desert, just as the Hebrew prophets had foretold. They remained buried and largely forgotten for more than 2,000 years.

The Babylonians aided the Medes in the conquest of Nineveh. The Babylonian general Nabopolassar founded a Chaldean dynasty that lasted less than a century. His son, Nebuchadnezzar, carried Babylonian conquests to the border of Egypt and, in 586 B.C., destroyed Jerusalem. Largely because of this act, Nebuchadnezzar has come down to us as a warrior, but he was known in his own time for peaceful accomplishments, such as the building of roads, canals, and temples. Babylon did not long outlast Nineveh. Cyrus, the King of the Persians, successors in power to the Medes, invaded in 539 B.C. When the walls of the city fell and Cyrus entered Babylon, its power came to an end forever. Like Nineveh, it became a symbol of grandeur turned to dust, one of the sinful cities of the Bible upon which God had visited a just destruction.

77

III

When the Semitic nomads settled in Mesopotamia, they absorbed much of the Sumerian civilization, already at a highly developed stage. In time, Mesopotamia became a cultural center, developing and sending forth ideas in science, mythology, and literature. These ideas were recorded in a system of writing we call cuneiform, set down on soft clay which was then baked hard. In the past 100 years so many tablets and cylinders with cuneiform writing have been unearthed that even today all of them have not been translated.

The same system of writing (cuneiform) was used in Mesopotamia for both the Semitic and the Sumerian languages. The Semitic language, known as Akkadian, was the one used by the Babylonians and Assyrians. The system of writing, which was Sumerian in origin, was originally pictographic and evolved from drawings of objects. With the development of a stylus for writing and clay as a writing material, exact drawing and particularly the representation of curved lines became difficult. The drawings were reduced to stylized combinations of lines representing the ideas conveyed by the original pictographs. These ideograms led to the development of signs representing phonetic entities that corresponded to the pictures.

Phonetic writing in Mesopotamia was complex. The word for milk was *ga,* and the word for bear was *az. Gaz,* meaning to break, was written *ga-az,* using two ideograms that, in themselves, are unrelated to the concept of break. The invention of phonetic writing was a great step forward, but it brought numerous complications. Signs could be read ideographically or phonetically, according to their context, and most ideograms consisted of signs with more than one phonetic value. As scholars have known for years, the Mesopotamian system of writing was one of the most difficult used in ancient times.

Mesopotamian literature, art, and law were deeply affected by the local religion, which was polytheistic (having many gods). The deities were largely taken over from Sumerian deities. They included a supreme triad, Anu, Enlil, and Enki (or Ea), representing heaven, air, and earth. Another triad represented the sun, the moon, and Venus, the morning star. There was a storm-god, Adad, and a god of fire, Nusku. Perhaps the most famous of the many deities was Ishtar, a fertility goddess symbolic of mother earth. A whole series of myths grew up around her, particularly in her manifestation as the goddess of love. Ashur in Assyria and Marduk in Babylon were worshiped as national gods, Marduk becoming preeminent in Babylon under Hammurabi.

Mesopotamian life was filled with the fear of demons. These were usually ghosts or evil spirits from beneath the earth, against whom men were defenseless. Curing disease, by and large, meant ridding a person of demons. The art of the period abounds with demons, figures that mix human and animal heads and bodies or terrifying combinations of animals. The use of spells and magic to

79

exorcise demons was widespread. One of the popular forms of magic was divination, trying to foretell the future by reading signs in certain objects. Mesopotamian diviners were particularly fond of examining the livers of animals.

Another form of divination was astrology, which, especially during the Chaldean period, gave rise to the more scientific study of astronomy. The astronomical data compiled by the ancient Mesopotamians was extensive. They worked out numerous astronomical tables, measured the course of various stars, plotted the movements of the sun and moon, and predicted eclipses. They also developed a calendar and advanced man's knowledge of mathematics. Their scientific legacy is still with us in part; among other things, names they gave to many constellations were taken over by the Greeks and are still afixed to modern sky charts.

IV

Unlike the Egyptians, the Mesopotamians produced a rich and influential body of literature. Its foundation is mythological, again a legacy from the Sumerians, and the great religious epics that have survived recount myths of the gods. They are concerned largely with the creation of the universe and man's ultimate destiny, the themes that begin and end our Bible.

The Creation myth is contained in an Akkadian epic called *Enūma eliš* (When on High), so named from its opening words. It tells how the chief god, Marduk, fashions heaven and earth and then man. A famous myth on the cycle of the seasons tells how Ishtar, the goddess of love, descends into the underworld, leaving one of her garments at each gate. The absence of love stops all reproduction on earth. When the gods plead with the queen of the underworld, Ishtar is sprinkled with the water of life and is allowed to depart. She recovers each of her garments as she returns, and life is renewed on earth.

The masterpiece of the ancient literature is the Gilgamesh Epic, a hero myth more ancient than the *Enūma elish* and one that spread beyond the borders of Mesopotamia. The story, which reflects man's search for immortality, is not entirely mythical—there was an actual Gilgamesh, King of Uruk. Gilgamesh, in the story, has seen all things, knows the hidden mysteries, and has discovered the secret of wisdom. After numerous adventures, in one of which he rejects the love of Ishtar, he is tormented by the death of his friend Enkidu. Realizing that he too must die, Gilgamesh seeks immortality. He goes to visit the old sage Utnapishtim, who gained immortality at the time of the Great Flood. Unable to attain immortality himself, Gilgamesh speaks to the ghost of Enkidu about life beyond the grave. It is on this gloomy note that the epic ends. Obviously, the striking feature of this epic to modern readers is the account of the Flood, which resembles that in the Bible to a remarkable degree.

Mesopotamian literature covers a wide range. In addition to religious epics, such as the *Enūma elish,* and heroic epics, such as the story of Gilgamesh, many religious lyrics—hymns, psalms and prayers, including a Mesopotamian Book of Job—have been uncovered. Prose writing, too, was religious, and we have many ritual texts on hand, descriptions of procedures and ceremonies, including that of a New Year celebration at Babylon. There are also numerous spells and incantations, as well as historical chronicles and dictionaries. Finally, there is a great body of scientific works—treatises on astronomy, mathematics, geography, medicine, chemistry, zoology, and botany.

V

The laws that governed Mesopotamian society were a fusion of Sumerian and Semitic elements. The famous Code of Hammurabi was discovered early in the twentieth century in the ruins of Susa, but it was carried there after an invasion of Babylon. It is not an original set of laws, as was first thought, but a codification of earlier, largely Sumerian, laws. However, as set down by Hammurabi, it spread widely and was influential on practically all subsequent legislation.

From the Code of Hammurabi we have learned that there were three levels of society in Babylonia—*awìlum* (patricians), *mushkénum* (citizens), and *wardum* (slaves). The Assyrians also had three classes, patricians,

82

slaves, and a middle class, whose status is not certain. The wealth of clay documents that have been uncovered tell us a great deal about life in ancient Mesopotamia. Many of the Babylonian documents are contracts, and they reveal a highly developed commercial life.

The principal occupation of the area was agriculture. Babylonia grew barley and other cereals, as well as sesame for its oil, and mulberries and pomegranates. The date palms of Babylonia were a great source of wealth. On the other hand, Assyria produced timber and stone. Because there was no stone in Babylonia, brickmaking was its principal industry. We also have records of winemaking and dairy farming. Trade was carried on by water and by caravan and extended through the Middle East and as far away as India. Merchants used rafts to transport stone downriver from Assyria. When they sold their stone, they dismantled their rafts to sell the timber, equally scarce in Babylonia, and returned north by caravan.

The Babylonian Code, though not as mild as the Sumerian or as harsh as the Assyrian, was based on retaliation. "An eye for an eye and a tooth for a tooth" was not a mere saying, but a fixed principle of law. Cases were tried in court before a judge who was appointed by the king, and his sentence was binding. The king was the supreme legal and religious authority. At first the kings were considered divine, but later they served as representatives of the gods.

Royal palaces grew to become cities within cities,

peopled by ministers, officials, overseers, workmen, priests, and countless lesser persons. Though the king was supreme, in Assyria the prime minister and the commander in chief of the army were important figures. The army was a highly developed limb of the government body. Soldiers fought with bows and arrows, lances, and battle-axes. They conducted sieges much the same way soldiers did in medieval times, relied heavily on chariots when they swept out in a path of conquest, and also made use of warships. Many examples of Assyrian palace art are concerned with scenes of war or with the hunting of wild animals.

VI

Monumental is the word for Assyrian and Babylonian art. It was traditional in form, and only in pictures and statues of animals does a spirit of dramatic realism shine through the formal style. The great palaces and towers impressed by their majestic massiveness, not through any elegance or grace of line. Statues were often enormous, and bas-reliefs, sculptures raised only slightly from a flat surface, might cover the face of a mountain.

Clay was plentiful, and construction was usually in brick. This turned out to be fortunate for archaeologists 2,000 years later. For one thing, stone buildings would have been quarried by the later settlers on the ruined sites. More important, when a brick building falls into ruin, the upper portion collapses first and covers the lower portion, helping preserve it intact. In this way, many fortresses, palaces, and temples remained for future excavators.

Temples were of two kinds, low and high. The more familiar high temples are known to us as ziggurats, or temple towers. They are terraced pyramids, with from three to seven "decks," each level smaller than the one below it. The most famous, called Etemenanki, was in Babylon. Statuary was not common, and the best known and most frequently found examples of sculpture are massive bas-reliefs, usually lions, bulls, and fantastic animals.

Few examples of painting have survived, but countless examples remain of something more utilitarian—the seal. Making seals was a form of bas-relief sculpture. Seals were used for personal identification marks, and documents were signed with seals. Mesopotamian seals were cylinders, on the curved surfaces of which were engraved scenes or inscriptions or, more often, both. A flat impression was obtained by rolling the cylinder over a surface of soft clay. In many cases, the seal had a hole bored through the axis, through which a string was passed, so that the owner could wear it suspended from his neck. Far less impressive than the monumental sculptures, the seals that have been unearthed in such vast quantities have actually contributed more to our modern understanding of the ancient Mesopotamian civilization.

Chapter Nine

Bird Tracks in the Sand

I

When Xenophon and the Ten Thousand, an army of Greek mercenaries, passed the remains of Nineveh, they had no idea what the ruins were. This was only 200 years after the destruction of the city. In A.D. 150 the Greek satirist Lucian wrote, "Nineveh has perished. No trace of it remains, and one would never know that it had existed." In the 1760's Karsten Niebuhr, a scholar from Copenhagen traveling in the Near East, saw the mounds at the site of the old city and thought they were natural hills.

The absence of visible relics played a significant part in the development of Mesopotamian archaeology. Travelers to the region found no temples, as in Greece, or pyramids, as in Egypt, only a flatland with mysterious mounds rising out of the dusty plain. These mounds, called tells, were actually gigantic piles of crumbling brick and broken pottery, covered over with centuries-old deposits of dirt. But to the passing observer the ancient kingdoms were as good as obliterated. In addition, the languages spoken by the natives of the region bore no relation to those once spoken there.

Actually, the ancient language was known to scholars, even though no archaeological ruins had been uncovered to show who the people were who used it or how they had lived. The key to cuneiform, the written form of the language, was discovered before the ancient Assyrian, Babylonian, and Sumerian civilizations were dug up. However, lack of enough samples to work from prevented scholars from gaining a full knowledge of the ancient language. For a long time, moreover, there was no general agreement among scholars that the few existing samples were actually writing. To those who refused to believe that the cuneiform inscriptions represented a language, they were merly decorative markings. And one observer said they looked as if birds had been walking over wet sand.

Not enough facts and too much fancy hampered the early study of ancient Mesopotamia. Insufficient knowledge of the different civilizations that had flourished in the area was one stumbling block; another was the fact that different forms of cuneiform had been used by the different peoples. From the start, two sites were known to scholars—the mountainside monument at Behistun and the ruins of Persepolis. The Arabs who had conquered the area paid no attention to Behistun or Persepolis, and legends that bore no relation to actuality grew up around them. The Behistun monument, carved by

Darius to proclaim his might, was identified as many other things, including a scene depicting a schoolmaster and his pupils. Persepolis was linked to King Solomon, though ancient writers had associated it with Darius and his successors. But facts about it were lost or garbled with the passing of time. Even its Persian name was lost, Persepolis being what the Greeks called it.

Travelers to Mesopotamia brought reports back to Europe as early as the twelfth century. Benjamin of Tudela, who traveled to Mosul from Spain, noted correctly that Mosul lay across the river from Nineveh. Leonhart Rauwolff, a German visitor in 1575, described the "high round hill" outside Mosul and wrote, "At that place and in the region hereabouts years ago the mighty city of Nineveh was situated." Sir Anthony Shirley, an Elizabethan traveler, also correctly identified Nineveh, but these observant travelers were matched by more imaginative reporters.

II

Mesopotamian archaeology began with a blighted love affair. Pietro della Valle (1586–1652) was a member of a noble Roman family. Disappointed in a love affair, he thought of committing suicide but decided instead to make a pilgrimage to the Holy Land. He then expanded his plans to include a tour of the Near East. Leaving Italy in 1614 for Constantinople, he spent a year studying Turkish and Arabic. In 1615 he was in Alexandria and Cairo, and a year later in the Holy Land. From there he traveled eastward through Persia, finally reaching India in 1623. After a year's stay he moved on to Basra and Aleppo, arriving back in Rome in 1626. Afterward he wrote extensively about his twelve years of travel in the Near East.

One of the places he visited was Takht-i-Jamshid (Persepolis). In the seventeenth century identifying the ruins of Jamshid was a subject for much argument. The fires of the argument were fueled by the inscriptions found there. Some of these had been copied and were described as a language "not Chaldean, nor Hebrew, nor Greek, nor Arabic, nor of any other known nation." Pietro della Valle was fascinated by these inscriptions, which he had seen elsewhere on little "bricks" and which he had collected. He recognized that the inscriptions were indeed a form of writing and sent one of his "bricks" to the Kircherian Museum. It was the first cuneiform document placed in a European museum.

One of the earliest theorizers about these inscriptions was Jean Chardin, a seventeenth-century Frenchman-turned-Englishman who later became Sir John Chardin. A traveler in the Orient who built a fortune trading in jewels, he settled in England in 1681, where he became court jeweler and was knighted by Charles II. Chardin wrote about his travels and discoveries in Persia, and he too considered the mysterious inscriptions a form of writing. He believed that this writing ran from left to right, as it does, and also perpendicularly, as it does not.

His confusion arose from having examined a set of characters that ran around a doorframe. Actually, what Chardin did not know—and what no one else knew at the time—was that the inscriptions were also in three separate languages using the same characters—Elamite, Old Persian, and Akkadian, running in this way

OLD PERSIAN

ELAMITE

AKKADIAN

A German doctor named Engelbert Kämpfer, who also copied the mysterious inscriptions, first recognized that their basic unit was a wedge. It was Kämpfer who named the writing cuneiform, which means wedge-shaped. The next advance came from Samuel Flower, who introduced the helpful aid of separating each sign by a dot. After him came Cornelias le Brun, who demonstrated that the upright inscriptions were not meant to be read vertically.

The first accurate copies of cuneiform were made by Karsten Niebuhr, who traveled in the Near East from 1760 to 1767. Niebuhr's book, *Description of Travels in Arabia and Adjacent Lands,* was kept close at hand by Bonaparte throughout his Egyptian campaign. Niebuhr noted that the inscriptions usually occurred in groups of three but did not realize that they were trilingual texts.

In copying the inscriptions, he used Samuel Flower's system of dots to separate signs but failed to realize that a constantly recurring symbol was actually a word divider. Niebuhr, who confirmed that the writing was read from left to right and horizontally, laid the foundation for the decipherment of cuneiform.

Niebuhr visited the gigantic ruins at Takht-i-Jamshid, which he correctly identified as the remains of Persepolis. Because his accurate copies of cuneiform, the first to circulate in Europe, were from Persepolis, the earliest efforts at decipherment concern the later Persepolitan cuneiform and not the Assyrian or Babylonian form. But these early efforts provided a key to deciphering the cuneiform that emerged years later from the ruins of the older civilizations.

The next development that proved helpful was the publication in Paris, in 1771, of Abraham Hyacinthe Anquetil-Duperron's translation of the Zend-Avesta, a collection of religious writings. Another helpful publication from Paris, in 1793, was Silvestre de Sacy's *Mémoires sur diverses antiquités de Perse,* which contained translations of the Greek versions of inscriptions at Naksh-i-Rustam. Equally helpful was De Sacy's contention that where inscriptions appeared over the figure of a ruler, they referred to him and his father and contained the phrase "king of kings."

The scholar O. G. Tychsen, in his book *De cuneatis inscriptionibus Persepolitanis lucubratio* (1798), identified the three scripts noted by Niebuhr as three separate languages, which he named Parthian, Median, and Bactrian. Tychsen studied an often-repeated group of seven signs which was frequently followed by a group of four signs. He announced that the first group represented the name of a ruler and that the second group meant pius or some such designation. From this theory he went on to many others, all of them guesses and all of them wrong. But his theories prompted another scholar to explore further and develop more clues.

F. C. C. Münter, in a paper read to the Royal Academy at Copenhagen in 1798, demonstrated that Tychsen was wrong about such things as his identification of the ruins at Takht-i-Jamshid. Münter, agreeing with Niebuhr, showed that the palace at Jamshid was actually Persepolis. He also first noted that a frequently occurring diagonal wedge in the cuneiform inscriptions was a word divider. Next, he launched into a study of Niebuhr's copies to find the other most frequent signs, which he felt would prove to be vowels. Though he wrongly identified five vowels and six consonants, he was correct in identifying *a* and *b*.

Münter also disagreed with Tychsen about his designation of pius. He felt that the seven-character grouping meant king and was not someone's name. The double grouping, seven characters plus four characters, he read as "king of kings." Thus, the grouping *before* the seven-character group would be a name. Münter was actually on the right track, but was thrown off by an unfortunate mistake. One of Niebuhr's rare errors in transcription made what should have been a royal name too short to work as such. Niebuhr had put in the word-divider sign where a letter should have gone. The first real step in decipherment was thus delayed, and the discovery of the key to cuneiform fell to someone who was really an amateur scholar.

III

Georg Friedrich Grotefend, who found the key to cuneiform, was no Champollion. Born in Münden, Germany, on June 9, 1775, Grotefend studied philology at Göttingen and became a schoolteacher there. When only twenty-seven, he discovered the way to decipher cuneiform in order to win a bet, and he worked largely by hunch, backed by limited knowledge. His method of attack was a masterpiece of shrewd and inspired reasoning; behind it was his study of the theories of his predecessors.

First, Grotefend noted, as Niebuhr had done earlier, that there were three different kinds of inscriptions at Persepolis. Knowing that Cyrus, a Persian, had conquered Babylonia about 540 B.C., he assumed that one script was Old Persian. Most likely, thought Grotefend, it was the middle of the three columns of writing, following a practice common in the Near East. Moreover, because fewer signs were used, he assumed that the middle inscription was alphabetic and not syllabic.

Next, he observed that a' group of signs and a single

93

sign reappeared frequently. The group, he decided, stood for king, and the single sign was a word divider. The next thing he determined, from the absence of curved lines, was that the characters had been impressed into the clay, not written. Then he studied the arrangement of the characters and noted that the points of the wedges faced either downward or to the right and that the angles consistently opened to the right.

Grotefend further assumed that inscriptions from monuments would have certain mannerisms and recurring phrases. Because the recurring group he had observed was, he felt, the word "king," he began to look for the configuration

(name), Great King, King of Kings; King of (name)
and (name); son of (name), Great King, King of Kings.

He also felt that this formula should appear in all three inscriptions. A diligent study of the inscriptions he had at hand produced appropriate configurations, thus supporting his theory.

What Grotefend also found were name groupings in close conjunction, suggesting a father-son relationship, and another name unaccompanied by the sign he read as "king." This set of character groups, he felt, produced another formula:

King B, son of A.
King C, son of King B.

In other words, he had discovered three persons, A, B, and C, who were grandfather, father, and son; the grand-

father was not a king, but the father and son were. Grotefend checked the available lists of royal successions for
two kings who would fit the formula. They could not be
Cyrus and Cambyses, he decided, because the initial
signs of the names were different. Nor could they be Cyrus and Artaxerxes, because the lengths of the names
were not so different in the cuneiform inscriptions. The
only names left to choose from were Darius and Xerxes.
This supposition was confirmed by the grandfather-father-
son relationship, because the grandfather in this case was
not a king.

Grotefend worked from two separate inscriptions
copied by Niebuhr and found the phrase "king of kings"
in both. He also found, in the first line of each inscription, a configuration without the "of kings" grouping but
followed by another word. This word, the same in both
inscriptions, he surmised to be "great." Thus, he had
worked out the phrase "king great" or "great king." A
name appeared before the "great king" configuration, but
it was a different name in each inscription. However, one
of the names appeared later accompanied by signs he
read as "son." Thus, inspired reasoning, not guesswork,
and some knowledge of earlier scholarship led Grotefend
to decipher cuneiform and read three names of the royal
house of Achaemenes:

Darius, Great King, King of Kings . . . son of Hystaspes.
Xerxes, Great King, King of Kings . . . son of King Darius.

The key to deciphering cuneiform was discovered by
Grotefend, but the glory such a discovery deserved was

not fully bestowed upon him. His theories were not widely accepted, though they were amplified and improved thirty years later by the Frenchman Eugène Burnouf and the Norwegian Christian Lassen. One reason for Grotefend's lack of fame is that his accomplishment was eclipsed by the work of Colonel Henry Rawlinson, an Englishman whose achievements were much more spectacular. Rawlinson, working independently many years later, also solved the riddle of cuneiform. His work was more widely known, and he also made many widely publicized discoveries of cuneiform texts. Fickle fame attached itself to the colorful Englishman, and the study of cuneiform stemmed from the work of Rawlinson, rather than that of Grotefend.

IV

Having worked out his theory, Grotefend then assigned phonetic values to the signs in the royal names he had identified. These names were known, and are still presented, in their Greek forms. Grotefend turned to the Zend-Avesta, where Antiquil-Duperron listed Hystaspes four different ways—Goshtasp, Gustasp, Kistasp, and Wistasp. Grotefend chose the first version. Studying the signs in the name he identified with Darius, he worked out *Darheush* as the pronunciation. We now know that the proper form is *Daryavush,* but Grotefend had deciphered four of the signs correctly—*d, a, r* and *sh.* From Herodotus, a questionable source, he learned that the name Xerxes was derived from the word "warrior," which he equated with "king," because the first two signs were the same as in the configuration he felt was Xerxes' name. Deciding that the first sign was *kh,* he arrived at KH*SH*H*A* R*SH*A, though we now know that it should have been KH*SH*Y*A*R*SH*A.

Working much the way Champollion was later to do with the Cleopatra and Ptolemy cartouches, Grotefend confirmed his theorizing by comparing the three names. The signs that should repeat were indeed similar in each of the names:

G * O * SH * T * A * S * P

D * A * R * H * E * U * SH

KH * SH * H * A * R * SH * A

The four signs were written

$$ \text{𐎺} = \text{SH} \quad \text{𐎫} = \text{A} \quad \text{𐎼} = \text{R} \quad \text{𐎹} = \text{H} $$

though the last one was actually *Y,* not *H.* In time he worked out phonetic values for thirteen cuneiform signs, though one (*A*) had been previously assigned by Münter, and four were later proved incorrect.

This was an outstanding achievement, particularly in 1802, and it was hailed by De Sacy, who published Grotefend's findings in an article the following year. But many authorities denied the value of his work, probably because he was a mere schoolteacher. He later studied another inscription, and by 1815, when fourteen cuneiform signs were deciphered, twelve had been worked out by Grotefend. But many of his papers and articles were ignored. They were uncovered and circulated widely for the first time in 1893, forty years after his death. His later efforts never matched his early triumph; they yielded little, and his attempts at translation were mere guesswork.

The science of Assyriology, so named because the early major discoveries were of Assyrian relics, and the study of cuneiform developed separately from the accomplishments of Grotefend. The study of Mesopotamian antiquities was first organized by C. J. Rich, an Englishman sent to Baghdad by the East India Company in 1808. Rich, who investigated and surveyed the sites of Babylon and Nineveh, collected numerous tablets and cylinders which were sent after his death to the British Museum.

After Grotefend, scholars proceeded slowly with the translation of cuneiform, spending much time disputing one another's findings. A French Orientalist, J. S. Saint-Martin, was critical of Grotefend and offered a different alphabet of his own. But where he differed from the schoolteacher he was almost always wrong, and all he contributed was two phonetic values. Rasmus Christian Rask, a distinguished Danish scholar and pioneer of comparative philology, corrected Grotefend's reading of

A*TSCH*A*O to A*N*A*M, thus adding two more signs to the list of those deciphered. Rask also demonstrated that the Zend-Avesta was really much older than most scholars believed it to be.

Eugène Burnouf, the foremost Zend scholar of his day, improved on the unreliable Zend-Avesta translation, uncovered trilingual texts, and corrected Grotefend's findings. He also worked on a Niebuhr inscription filled with proper names, a list of twenty-four Persian provinces. Burnouf identified sixteen, but only half of them correctly. He claimed to have deciphered twelve signs, but eight were later proved incorrect, and two were already known. So he, too, added only two signs to the slowly growing list. However, when the Norwegian Christian Lassen, a friend of Burnouf's, correctly identified twenty of the twenty-four provinces in Niebuhr's Persepolitan inscription, he added eight signs to the list.

Not enough examples of the language existed for complete study. One available source, however, had not been tapped. Darius' inscription on the Rock of Behistun contained 1,000 lines of writing, ten times as much as all the other known material combined. Only when this monumental message was copied and deciphered would the way be open to study cuneiform. It was copied, a feat involving incredible gymnastics and nerves of iron, and it was deciphered. One man accomplished both tasks, the same man who overshadowed Grotefend—Henry Rawlinson.

Chapter Ten

The Daring Diplomats

I

There it stood, more than 200 feet above the ancient road from Hamadan to Babylon, an enormous bas-relief surrounded by columns of writing, carved into the side of a mountain. There it stood, for more than 2,000 years proclaiming the might of Darius to passing strangers who no longer understood or cared about its message. There it stood, the Rock of Behistun, an abundant source of cuneiform inscriptions waiting for a translator, a man athletic enough, adventurous enough, and learned enough to tackle the job—a man like Rawlinson.

Henry Creswicke Rawlinson was one of the special breed of scholarly adventurers who made nineteenth-century archaeology so colorful. And like so many of his fellows, he was an amateur archaeologist, though an extremely well-versed one. Rawlinson was born in 1810

100

and entered the military service of the East India Company in 1826. As a cadet aboard a ship bound for India he met and became friendly with Sir John Malcolm, the governor of Bombay and a prominent Orientalist. Sir John spent much of the voyage talking to the young man and filled him with his own deep and passionate interest in Persian history and literature. By 1833 Rawlinson was a major on duty in Persia; ten years later he was British consul in Baghdad. Subsequently he became a lieutenant colonel, a director of the East India Company, a Member of Parliament, and British minister to Persia. But it is not for this distinguished career that he is remembered.

In 1835, having studied Persian, Rawlinson was one of a select group of officers sent to Kermanshah as military advisers to the brother of the shah. On the way to this post, he stopped at Mount Elvand to copy two cuneiform inscriptions that had not yet been published. Though he read of various Mesopotamian studies and knew that the names of three Achaemenians had been identified, he was at this time unaware of Grotefend's feat of decipherment. Thus, thirty years after the German schoolteacher, he duplicated Grotefend's theorizing and deciphered the three names. When, in 1836, he discovered Grotefend's work, he realized that he had improved on the German's methods and was further advanced in the study of cuneiform. He also realized that the principal need of any scholar in the field was for more inscriptions that contained names. Such inscriptions, he knew, were twenty miles away.

101

Darius' memorial at Behistun had been known for centuries, even if it had been largely ignored. Carved high on the sheer face of a mountain that rose nearly 2,000 feet, it was hard to miss; in fact, Darius had chosen the site because it was prominent, to commemorate his victory over a group of rebels nearly 2,500 years ago. It consists of a sculptured scene with fourteen columns of writing at its sides and beneath it in three languages which we now know are Old Persian, Elamite, and Babylonian. The bas-relief depicts fourteen figures; one, wearing a crown, is obviously a king. He is accompanied by two armed attendants, and his right hand is raised to a heavenly figure (Ahura-Mazda) who returns the salute. The king's left foot rests on the body of a prostrate prisoner whose arms are raised in an appeal for mercy. Nine captives, their hands bound behind their backs, stand in line before the king, linked by a rope around their necks. In addition to the texts around this scene, there are inscriptions above and below the figures.

For months, throughout 1837, Rawlinson came to Behistun whenever he was able to leave Kermanshah for a few hours. He found it not too difficult to climb up to the memorial, which he measured as 150 feet wide and 100 feet high. Standing on the narrow ledge at its base, he was directly in front of the five columns of Old Persian text, containing more than 400 lines of writing. These he could copy, and did, though he worked with a sheer drop of more than 200 feet immediately behind his back. Starting with thirteen signs he had deciphered from the Mount Elvand inscriptions, he worked out A * R * SH * A * M, a name which he identified with the Greek Arsames. This gave him the *M,* which helped him decipher another name. Soon he had worked out the names for Persia, Achaemenian, Babylon, and Euphrates and had deciphered eighteen characters.

Late in the year, having copied more than 200 lines of Old Persian, he began a translation of the opening paragraphs of the text. This he submitted to the Royal Asiatic Society in London, in a paper which presented the text as he had copied it, a transliteration, and then his translation. It was received in 1838 and was copied and sent to Paris, where it excited great interest. Rawlinson was made an honorary member of the French Asiatic Society and was put in touch with Burnouf and Lassen and notified of the work being done by other scholars.

Rawlinson's duties removed him from the area for a time, but he returned to Behistun in 1844. In order to copy all the Old Persian, he had to be lowered by block and tackle from the top of the mountain, working his way down the face of the cliff. In succeeding years, as he worked at the other texts, Rawlinson resorted to using ladders, cables, hooks, and other equipment, sometimes at the risk of his life. In 1847 he relied on an extremely agile Kurdish boy to help him obtain squeezes (impressions) of hard-to-reach inscriptions. The boy swung from ropes anchored to stakes driven into cracks in the mountainside, rode in a harnesslike cradle, and even crawled across the face of the memorial, hanging on by his toes and fingertips. It seems unjust that fifty years later the squeezes he obtained should be partially destroyed when mice in the British Museum nibbled at them.

II

Scholars classified the three languages using cuneiform writing as Class I, Class II, and Class III. Rawlinson and Grotefend had both worked on the Class I texts of the trilingual Behistun and Persepolis inscriptions. By 1846, with their work and that of a German scholar named Adolf Holtzmann, plus the contributions of an Irish clergyman, Edward Hincks, all the sign values of Class I, Old Persian, were virtually assigned. Scholars could turn their attention to Class II, which the Dane Niels Westergaard did for the next eight years, and to Class III. Advances were made in Class III study by a Swede, Löwenstern, but the most significant development came from the desk of the Reverend Edward Hincks. It was this quiet, bespectacled clergyman, a discoverer without undertaking any excavations, who showed that Babylonian contained no letters as such but was made up of consonant-vowel, vowel-consonant, and consonant-vowel-consonant combinations. Hincks also showed that a single sign could be an ideogram, a syllable, or a determinative.

This distressing discovery came at the time that another scholar entered the field of Mesopotamian studies.

Jules Oppert, a German-born French Orientalist and professor of Sanskrit, abandoned ancient India for a subject he found more fascinating and was, by 1852, excavating in Mesopotamia. Some years before, he had begun sharing studies with Rawlinson, and the two worked together on deciphering the Class III texts, having become good friends.

While working on Class III writing, Rawlinson, like Hincks, realized that this version differed significantly from Class I, which was an alphabetical script. In Class I each sign stood for a sound; but in Class III, it turned out, a sign might stand for a syllable or a whole word, and the same sign, moreover, might represent several different syllables or several different words. Also, it was discovered, several signs might express the same word. The difficulties facing Rawlinson and the other scholars may be seen in the problems related to the sound *r*. The *r* sound was actually expressed by six different signs, depending upon whether it was indicating *ra, ri, ru, ar, ir,* or *ur*. When a consonant was added—*m*, for example, producing either *mar* or *ram*—an entirely new ideogram resulted. Furthermore, the pronunciation of the new ideogram could not be deduced from its components.

Then, unexpectedly, a most fortunate discovery was made at the excavations at Kuyunjik. Among many clay tablets uncovered there, about 100 dating from the seventh century B.C., proved to be a virtual dictionary. They contained comparative lists in which the phonetic values, and meanings of ideograms were correlated to the alpha-

105

betical script. On some tablets Sumerian and Semitic equivalents were listed; on others, pictures of objects were arranged in rows labeled with their Sumerian and Semitic names. The Sumerian language had not been identified as such, there having been no excavation as yet of the Sumerian culture, but its relation to Class III writing seemed clear to Rawlinson.

Despite the virtual decipherment of Class I writing and Rawlinson's identification, with the aid of the Persian text, of about 500 words of Class III, as well as work on Class II, there was considerable controversy in the 1850's about the ability to read the various forms of cuneiform. To certain scholars, the claims and theories of Rawlinson and the other decipherers were unsupported. A mathematician and pioneer in photography, William Henry Fox Talbot, devised a test that would settle the controversy once and for all. He persuaded the Royal Asiatic Society in London to send copies of a newly discovered Assyrian inscription, separately and in sealed envelopes, to three of the leading cuneiform experts for decipherment. Copies went to Rawlinson, Hincks, and Oppert, and a fourth copy was taken by Talbot himself. Each man worked independently and in his own way, not knowing what the other three were doing, and returned his translation in a sealed envelope to the society. When the results of this test were examined by the society, it was found that all four versions agreed on all essential points. The publication in 1857 of *An Inscription by Tiglath-pileser, King of Assyria, Translated by Rawlinson, Talbot, Dr. Hincks, and Op-*

pert, stilled the controversy and proved that cuneiform was decipherable.

III

In Egypt many monuments of the past and examples of hieroglyphics were readily at hand; in Mesopotamia almost everything had to be unearthed. The study of cuneiform was dependent on digging up sufficient samples for the scholars to work on. Thus, along with Rawlinson, two excavators, Botta and Layard, have made their names an essential part of the story of cuneiform. Like Rawlinson, they were government agents for whom archaeology was a passionate avocation, not their principal occupation.

Paul Émile Botta was a physician who had traveled around the world and settled in Egypt. In 1833 the French government named him consul in Alexandria, but in 1840 he was appointed consular agent in Mosul and moved to that city on the upper Tigris. A scientist and linguist, as well as a diplomat, Botta familiarized himself with the native languages wherever he went. Soon he was on friendly terms with the inhabitants of Mosul and was buying antiquities from them. When asked, the natives said they didn't know where the articles came from; they were simply strewed around. Botta determined to gather antiquities on his own; this he decided meant digging for them. The site he chose for digging was an enormous mound at nearby Kuyunjik.

After a year of fruitless labor, an Arab who had

learned of his interest in ancient bricks with writing on them came to him and told him that such bricks and other antiquities could be found at Khorsabad, about ten miles away. Botta sent one of his diggers to investigate. A week later the man returned, reporting excitedly of walls covered with pictures and carvings of monsters and strange animals. Now Botta went to Khorsabad himself, and what he saw prompted him to bring his entire crew of diggers to the site. Soon he was able to share his own excitement with the whole world, as he announced that he had discovered a palace with sculptures "that can be truly identified with the period when Nineveh was at its height."

Twenty-four centuries of oblivion were about to be erased. The discovery made by Botta was tremendous, but as he was aware, the task he had started was even more tremendous. From the palace of Sargon, which is what he had uncovered, he wrote on May 2, 1843: "I sincerely regret being the only person on the spot to describe these ruins. I am no artist, and the sketches I transmit to you are not merely unworthy copies of the originals, but, further, they engross much of my time. Besides, I feel myself incompetent, through want of requisite learning, to appreciate the historic value of several details which, perhaps, might set others on the track to make interesting discoveries." He concluded with the first of several pleas for official support.

Botta, aware as he was of his insufficiencies, continued to report on his findings. "By making inquiries," he wrote from Mosul on July 24, 1843, "I have endeavored, but in vain, to learn whether this village had not anciently some other name of more Chaldean sound than Khorsabad or Khestéabad (for so it is still written): there is no local tradition on the subject, and even the inhabitants themselves were ignorant of the archaeological treasures lying buried under their feet, and which chance enabled me to discover; my researches shall continue notwithstanding." He closed with his repeated warning that many sculptures were deteriorating because they were exposed to the open air.

From 1843 to 1846 Botta continued to dig at Khorsabad, supported at last by help from France, but considerably harassed by the local Turkish pasha, who thought he had discovered gold. Professional archaeologists came to help dig away the palace, which they identified as a summer palace built outside Nineveh by King Sargon in 709 B.C. Numerous sculptures and bas-reliefs were uncovered, as well as weapons and everyday utensils. But much of what was uncovered crumbled when exposed to the sun and air. In answer to Botta's pleas, the French government sent the famous draftsman Eugène Napoléon Flandin to draw the various antiquities before they fell apart. Not everything that was uncovered deteriorated, and Botta sent magnificent sculptures back to the Louvre. Meanwhile, he went on digging, helped and eventually succeeded by a commission of nine archaeologists.

Among his helpers, for a time, was an Englishman

named Layard, whose own excavations would soon become even more famous. But Botta's place in the history of archaeology was secure. He uncovered, in a land written of in the Bible, something unsuspected—a culture as old as Egypt's. Much more work would be accomplished in Mesopotamia before this revelation could be confirmed, but Botta, who had started it all, would not be part of the later excavating. A change in government in France caused him to be sent to a minor post in North Africa. His archaeological discoveries had come to an abrupt end, but while they lasted, they had brought about a most important beginning.

IV

Many boys dream of growing up to lives of adventure because of the colorful things they read in books; few of them, as adults, succeed in making their dreams come true. Austen Henry Layard was one of the few. Though born in Paris in 1817 and educated in Italy, France, and Switzerland, he grew up in England, where his family settled. Layard studied law and eventually entered government service, becoming undersecretary for foreign affairs and later minister to Spain. But as with Rawlinson, it is not his governmental career that has made him famous. It is his dream-come-to-life for which Layard is remembered.

As a boy, his imagination spurred on by the stories he read in the *Arabian Nights,* he dreamed constantly of going to Baghdad, Damascus, and other colorful cities of the Near East. In 1839, scarcely more than into his manhood, he left his job in London and began to fulfill his dream. Before traveling in the Near East, however, he prepared himself in a practical manner. He carefully studied everything he thought would be of importance to him—from languages to first aid, from preparing topographical surveys to fighting tropical diseases. Only then did he proceed on his adventure.

Through most of 1839 and 1840, Layard and a single companion wandered through Syria and Asia Minor, visiting the famous sites and the few known archaeological ruins. They rode alone, their valises packed behind their saddles, protected only by the side arms they carried. Their only shelter at night was what they could find with the natives—tents and village huts. Desiring to see Mesopotamia, Layard left Aleppo on March 18, crossed the upper Euphrates, and arrived at Mosul on April 10, averaging about fifteen miles a day. At Mosul he visited the ruins on the east bank of the Tigris, believed to be those of Nineveh but, at the time, still unexplored and not positively identified.

From Mosul, Layard rode south to explore the vast mound at Kalah Shergat on the Tigris. On the way, he stopped for the night at the small Arab village of Hammum Ali, which was surrounded by vestiges of an ancient city. To the east he could see a line of lofty mounds; one of them, taller than the rest, was like a pyramid in shape. Layard recognized it as a pyramid described by

111

Xenophon, near which the Ten Thousand had encamped. The ruins around it had been described by the Greek general more than 2,200 years earlier as being, even then, those of an ancient city. In another intuitive identification, Layard said this was the city founded by Nimrod, "one of the first settlements of the human race."

He had time to examine the site only briefly. According to local tradition, strange figures carved in black stone were still present among the ruins, but Layard searched for them in vain. Though his visit was neither lengthy nor rewarding, it was memorable for Layard. He would afterward state that these mounds made a deeper impression on him than any other sites he visited. Lack of funds brought his first journey to a halt and forced him to return to Constantinople. But a few years later, financed by Sir Stratford Canning, the British ambassador to Constantinople, he was back. With Sir Stratford's gift of sixty pounds to help him, he began to explore the mound at Nimrud.

It would often be held up to Layard that luck was uncommonly with him in his endeavors, and indeed it was, but his excavations at Nimrud started on an unlucky note. A new pasha was governing the region, and the countryside was in open rebellion against him. This despot, moreover, did not look kindly upon foreigners. Layard, in order to disguise his intentions, announced he was hunting wild boar and rode off into the desert alone, armed with some rifles and a short spear. He quickly made friends with a local Bedouin sheikh named Awad, and hired six Arab workmen from him.

Roaming the mound at dawn, he selected a spot for the workmen to start digging. Within hours they found relics and soon after had dug a trench along a palace wall. Layard then sent three of the men to the other side of the mound, where almost at once they uncovered the corner walls of a second palace. Here was an early instance of his famous luck, but his own account of this discovery shows that there was more to his method than mere luck.

"Twenty minutes' walk," he wrote in *A Popular Account of Discoveries at Nineveh* (1851), "brought us to the principal mound. The absence of all vegetation enabled me to examine the remains with which it was covered. Broken pottery and fragments of bricks, both inscribed with cuneiform character, were strewed on all sides. The Arabs watched my motions as I wandered to and fro, and observed with surprise the objects I had collected. They joined, however, in the search, and brought me handfuls of rubbish, among which I found with joy the fragment of a bas-relief. The material on which it was carved had been exposed to fire, and resembled, in every respect, the burnt gypsum of Khorsabad. Convinced from this discovery, that sculptured remains must still exist in some part of the mound, I sought for a place where excavations might be commenced with a prospect of success. Awad led me to a piece of alabaster which appeared above the soil. We could not remove it, and on digging downward, it proved to be the upper part of a large slab. I ordered all the men to work around it, and they shortly uncovered a second slab. Continuing in the same line, we came upon a third; and, in the course of the morning, discovered ten more, the whole forming a square, with a slab missing at one corner. It was evident that we had entered a chamber, and that the gap was its entrance. I now dug down the face of one of the stones, and an inscription in the cuneiform character was soon exposed to view. Similar inscriptions occupied the center of all the slabs, which were in the best preservation; but plain, with the exception of the writing. Leaving half the workmen to remove the rubbish from the chamber, I led the rest to the S.W. corner of the mound, where I had observed many fragments of calcined alabaster."

Layard could not hide his activities from the pasha once gold-covered objects showed up at the dig. When that wily despot learned of the discovery, he sent soldiers to Nimrud ordering a halt in the excavations. Layard went to see the pasha, who claimed that the mound was an old Mohammedan burial ground and Layard's digging there was an act of sacrilege. When the stymied excavator returned to the site, he found that gravestones were indeed in evidence. But three days later, having won the confidence of the pasha's officer, he learned that the cunning tyrant was ordering his soldiers to dig up gravestones and plant them, under the cover of darkness, in the mound at Nimrud. At this point, Layard's

luck returned. The Turkish government suddenly recalled the pasha, and the digging resumed.

One day an excited workman came running up to
Layard, calling: "Hasten, O Bey, hasten to the diggers,
for they have found Nimrod himself." Following the awe-
struck Arab to the spot where the men were working,
Layard observed the great find they had made. "They
had uncovered the upper part of a figure," he later wrote,
"the remainder of which was still buried in the earth. I
saw at once that the head must belong to a winged
lion or bull, similar to those of Khorsabad and Persepolis. It was in admirable preservation. The expression
was calm yet majestic, and the outline of the features
showed a freedom and knowledge of art, scarcely to be
looked for in works of so remote a period. . . . I was
not surprised that the Arabs had been amazed and terri-
fied at this apparition. It required no stretch of imagination to conjure up the most strange fancies. This gigantic
head, blanched with age, thus rising from the bowels of
the earth, might well have belonged to one of those fear-
ful beings which are pictured in the traditions of the
country, as appearing to mortals, slowly ascending from
the regions below."

The find proved to be a gigantic sculptured head and
torso in alabaster of a winged lion. We now know that
it was one of the four gods identified with the cardinal
points of the compass; these were Marduk, a winged
bull; Nebo, a human figure; Nergal, a winged lion; and
Ninurta, an eagle. The discovery of what was reported

115

to be Nimrod himself excited the superstitious natives of the region and stirred every level of government up to the sultan in Constantinople. After some delay, the sultan gave Layard an official permit which allowed him to continue digging undisturbed. Soon thirteen pairs of winged lions and bulls were brought to light, and then a whole palace emerged slowly from the mound. We now know this to be the palace of King Ashurnasirpal II, who reigned from 885 to 859 B.C.

After sending enormous statues and bas-reliefs to the British Museum, Layard turned to the mound at Kuyunjik, where Botta had dug fruitlessly for a year. He began his excavations there in 1849, guided by signs his practiced eye detected and undaunted by claims that he was merely lucky and that his findings at Nimrud had been a fluke. Driving a vertical shaft into the mound, he hit bricks in twenty feet. Digging horizontally in several directions, he soon reached a large hall and then a gate flanked by winged bulls. In four weeks he uncovered nine chambers of a palace, later identified as that of Sennacherib (704–681 B.C.).

Layard revealed to the modern world the ancient city of Nineveh, which, before his excavations, had been more legendary than real, despite Rich's identification of it. For a period of less than a century, before its destruction in 612 B.C., Nineveh was so powerful a city, such a miracle of the ancient world, that the Biblical references have colored its history for all time. It remains, even now, the symbol of a sophisticated, pleasure-

116

mad, power-mad civilization dashed suddenly to a guilty and well-deserved destruction.

Layard's last great find was a "library" of nearly 30,000 clay tablets, among them the dictionary texts that helped in the decipherment of Class III cuneiform. The most important literary finds, however, were made by his assistant and successor, Hormuzd Rassam, who took over the excavations after Layard entered into his diplomatic career. It was Rassam who first uncovered the Gilgamesh Epic. But the discoveries made by Layard remain among the greatest accomplishments of nineteenth-century archaeology. In the span of a relatively few years, Layard, Botta, and Rawlinson revealed more about ancient Mesopotamia than had been known to the Greeks of more than 2,000 years ago.

Chapter Eleven

Legends Come to Life

I

The rediscovery of ancient civilizations often resembles the peeling of an onion, with different cultures being exposed, layer by layer, as the archaeologists dig deeper and farther back in time. The process reverses the march of history. People come to an area and settle it; a city grows up; invaders come and destroy the city; the sands of the desert or the dirt that accompanies desolation bury the ruins. New people come, drawn by the same attraction that lured the original settlers; the whole cycle repeats itself. In this way, cities and whole civilizations are built upon the ruins of earlier cities. The archaeologists, who start at the top layer and dig down, uncover the newer cultures before the older ones.

In Mesopotamia this process held especially true. Even the language revealed itself backward, the Persian version before the older ones, and Sumerian the last. But tracing the development of a language by working backward is not quite as easy as onion peeling. In the case of cuneiform there were complications that revealed themselves only as study progressed. Rawlinson became aware of some of the difficulties as he worked on Class III cuneiform. Difficulties of another sort were encountered by the scholars working on the Class II inscriptions.

Niels Ludvig Westergaard was a Danish scholar who visited Persia in 1843, searching for inscriptions. Two new ones that he found opened up serious study of Class II cuneiform, which we now call Elamite. One inscription was from Persepolis, the other was from the tomb of Darius at Naksh-i-Rustam. The Darius inscription contained a long list of lands he had conquered, which provided Westergaard with the proper names he needed to work from. He quickly deciphered the Elamite versions of Darius and Persia, as well as other proper nouns. What Westergaard did was to analyze sign groups in conjunction with their Old Persian equivalents. By this comparison method he obtained a list of sign values that allowed him to transliterate unfamiliar words. He concluded that the Class II writing was part syllabic and part alphabetic and estimated that it contained more than 100 characters, of which he identified more than 80.

By this time cuneiform scholarship was a truly international affair. Westergaard joined several other scholars in the study of the Behistun inscriptions that Rawlinson had copied. Rawlinson, meanwhile, turned over all his materials to Edwin Norris, assistant secretary of the Royal Asiatic Society in London, feeling that the other scholars were further advanced in the study of Class II. Norris deciphered most of Rawlinson's Class II texts by 1852. But deciphering Class II cuneiform did not unlock all its mysteries.

What was this language? Who were the people who had used it. Westergaard, following the suggestion of another scholar, called the language Median, but other scholars proposed the names Amardian and Susian. While this controversy raged, it was established that the language was built on a system of ninety-six syllabic sounds, representing consonant-vowel and consonant-vowel-consonant combinations, plus twenty-two ideograms and determinatives. Further study of inscriptions from Susa showed that the language was a development of that spoken by the people of Elam.

Meanwhile, the excavations of Botta and Layard had yielded a rich flow of inscriptions in a language closely resembling the third type of Achaemenian, which turned everyone's attention back to Behistun. When Rawlinson obtained his 112 lines of badly weathered text in 1847, through his own daring and that of his Kurdish helper, the relationships of the different versions of cuneiform were becoming clearer. Rawlinson recognized that Class III was similar to known Semitic dialects and, aided by the Persian version, proceeded with his decipherment.

By 1850 he had deciphered about 150 characters and determined the meaning of some 500 words.

At the same time, Hincks was publishing his own list of deciphered characters, including the vowels *a, e, i,* and *u* (there was no *o*). Hincks showed that many Assyrian signs were syllabic and identified ideographs and determinatives. Led by Hincks and Rawlinson, cuneiform studies advanced rapidly. Scholars could use the trilingual Achaemenian inscriptions to help them work on the unilingual ones from Babylonia and Assyria. Babylonian and Assyrian were recognized as being Semitic and closely related, though not identical. It was also recognized that two separate methods of writing existed in each region, but this complication did not deter the decipherers. The Royal Asiatic Society's test vindicated their efforts, but even the decipherment of all three forms of cuneiform did not clear up the mysteries lurking in that writing.

II

It had become apparent to the cuneiform scholars that some of the texts they were working with were in an unknown language and that this unknown language was not Semitic. It also became clear that the dictionary texts, the lexicons, and the phrase books that were included in the library of Ashurbanipal discovered by Layard were probably written to help Assyrian students of this unknown tongue. These dictionary texts made the meanings of this early language clear, though the grammar remains uncertain, but they left one question unanswered. Who spoke and wrote this language?

The possibility of an unknown civilization was raised —a non-Semitic people who had been in Mesopotamia before the Semites settled there. There was support for this notion in a reference to a very ancient King of Sumer and Akkad. Rawlinson suggested calling these early inhabitants Akkadians, but Jules Oppert said they should be called Sumerians, and his view prevailed. We now give the name Akkadian to the Semitic conquerors of the Sumerians and to their language.

The first actual remains of the Sumerians were excavated by the Frenchman Ernest de Sarzec, another amateur archaeologist. They were carvings in an unfamiliar style, dated by the scholars as having been done between 4000 and 3000 B.C., making their civilization older than that of Egypt. Sarzec began his excavations in 1877; these were followed by many more digs, chiefly by American and German archaeologists. The most famous of these digs, however, came in the 1920's, when Sir Leonard Woolley, at Ur, uncovered the city that was the legendary home of the Biblical patriarch Abraham.

It was many years before the different hypotheses about the Sumerians could be proven. Excavations at the site of ancient Uruk from 1928 to 1931 brought forth the discovery of picture writing in which each symbol represented a whole word. Meanwhile, other mounting archaeological evidence added enough information to permit a reconstruction of Sumerian history and culture. With this reconstruction came a clearer picture of how Sumerian writing developed and changed.

Originally, it had been picture writing that featured curved lines. The word "ox," for example, was

which is a clearly representational symbol. Originally, also, it was a form of writing arranged in vertical columns and read downward. But at some point it was recognized that script can be read more easily horizontally. With this discovery and the accompanying changeover, the writing altered accordingly, so that "ox" became   and inscriptions were written and read

from left to right.

The elimination of curved lines and the assumption of the wedgelike shape we associate with cuneiform came about when the stylus used for inscribing was altered. In early Babylonian, "ox" was   a recog-

nizable wedgelike variation on   The early wedge

symbols were gradually simplified; "ox" in Assyrian be-

123

came Meanwhile, the language was changing in structure, as well as appearance, the development of phonetic writing being aided by the monosyllabic nature of Sumerian words. The number of signs in use was reduced from about 2,000 to fewer than 700. At the same time, the Semitic conquerors adapted, as well as adopted, Sumerian usages and characters. They developed composite characters; for example, "water"

and "heaven" were combined to form "rain"

the "water of heaven." They also worked numerous Sumerian signs into their own syllables, in consonant-vowel, vowel-consonant, and consonant-vowel-consonant combinations.

But language was not the only legacy of the Sumerians. Their influence on law, mathematics, astronomy, architecture, and business was enormous and lasting. Much of what we associate with Babylonia's highly developed civilization was Sumerian in origin. Perhaps most important of all was the influence of Sumerian literature and legend. At a time when scholars and scientists were involved in a Bible-oriented controversy because of the work of Charles Darwin, the discovery of the Sumerian Creation and Flood stories threw Biblical study into further turmoil. These upsetting discoveries center on the work of still another amateur archaeologist.

III

George Smith, who was born in London in 1840, was a banknote engraver by profession. In his spare time he studied Assyriology and taught himself to read cuneiform. Unlike Grotefend, he was recognized and rewarded for his efforts. Learned papers he wrote brought him scholarly attention, and he was made an assistant in the Egyptian-Assyrian section of the British Museum. Eventually, he wrote twelve books before his untimely death at the age of thirty-six.

In 1872, while working at the British Museum on the deciphering of tablets sent back by Rassam, which Smith had grouped under the heading "Legends and Mythology," the young Englishman began to reconstruct the ·Gilgamesh Epic. Smith's recognition of what the tablets contained was instantaneous. "On looking down the third column," he later wrote, "my eye caught the statement that the ship rested on the mountains of Nizir, followed by the account of the sending forth of the dove, and its finding no resting-place and returning. I saw at once that I had here discovered a portion at least of the Chaldean account of the Deluge."

An important passage, estimated by Smith at fifteen

lines, was unfortunately missing from Rassam's collection of tablets. A London newspaper, the *Daily Telegraph,* offered 1,000 guineas to finance an expedition to Kuyunjik to find the missing portions of the Gilgamesh Epic. Smith himself led the expedition, which uncovered 384 tablets, including the missing fragment. It is a measure of Smith's skill that he found what he was looking for within a week and that the fragment turned out to be seventeen lines, only two more than he had estimated. Smith returned to the Middle East in 1874 on an expedition for the British Museum. He was back again in 1876, but while traveling in the desert, he died of dysentery. His career was brief, but fruitful, and his metamorphosis from banknote engraver to archaeologist marks him as a kind of tragic, yet splendid butterfly.

What Smith's discovery proved was that the Bible was more intimately bound up with the ancient history of the Semites than had been thought. If the uniqueness of the Bible was being questioned, its validity as a document of historical, archaeological, sociological, and anthropological importance was being strengthened. The studies by Smith and the findings of Layard and others were throwing new light on the importance of the Babylonians and their predecessors. The Gilgamesh Epic was not the only startling revelation contained in the Babylonian writings. Their Creation story was found to contain the familiar incident of woman arising from the rib of man. Even the name Eden derived from the Babylonians; their word for plain turned out to be *edinu.*

IV

After Layard, the treasure trove of Mesopotamian antiquities turned into a flood of its own. Where once Babylonian inscriptions had been available, as at Behistun, only as repetitions of Old Persian texts, now unilingual texts told their own story. There were not just royal memorial inscriptions, but thousands of examples of writing concerned with every aspect of Babylonian life—mortgages, contracts, account books, business notes, legal codes, government decrees, royal communications, myths, hymns, prayers, and all sorts of other documents from boundary markers to incantations. Moreover, passages in various documents linked recorded events to precise astronomical observations, allowing for positive dating of the events. And finally Babylon itself lay revealed—largely through the efforts of one man.

Robert Koldewey was a German art historian who took up archaeology and, in the 1880's, conducted digs in Mesopotamia and other areas. In 1898, at the age of forty-three, he began his excavations at Babylon. Early the following year he uncovered part of the city's famous walls. Babylon's wonders had been much written about. Herodotus described its enormous walls as being wide enough for two chariots to pass each other atop them. This was considered the usual exaggeration of a reporter known to be unreliable. Koldewey now had the opportunity to prove or disprove one of Babylon's legends.

But excavating in Babylon was not simple. The city, unlike Nineveh, had been rebuilt after its destruction; moreover, it had been inhabited for many more centuries than the Assyrian capital. Koldewey's efforts were slowed by an enormous pileup of centuries of rubble. His crews dug from 38 to 77 feet deep to reach important finds; with more than 200 workmen on the job, it took fifteen years to uncover the ancient city. But when they were done, it was apparent that Koldewey had uncovered the largest walled city of the ancient world.

One wall of brick was more than 22 feet thick; 38 feet outside it was another brick wall 25 feet thick; and there was also an inner brick wall 12 feet in thickness. The spaces between were filled with dirt and were wide enough to fit four horses abreast, confirming Herodotus. Koldewey also found watchtowers every 160 feet and estimated that there must have been 360 of them when the walls were intact. This discovery confirmed another classical account of Babylon that had been considered an exaggeration.

What Koldewey had found was the Babylon of Nebuchadnezzar. Where other cities and earlier structures on the same site had been built of perishable sun-dried brick, Nebuchadnezzar built his palaces and great buildings of durable kiln-baked brick. Unfortunately, this did not ensure that his city would last through the ages; rather, it prompted later builders in search of brick to

128

dismantle the ruins. The modern city of Hilla is built of bricks bearing Nebuchadnezzar's seal, and other similarly marked bricks from Babylon can be found in a nearby modern dam.

Koldewey's excavations revealed marvels of construction, such as the Ishtar Gate and a wide ceremonial avenue, that confirmed the legendary splendor of the ancient city. He also found a well with accompanying machinery and a structure that had once included a series of arches. This he felt certain was Nebuchadnezzar's Hanging Gardens, one of the Seven Wonders of the World. Then he uncovered the base of a great tower, a structure in the shape of a step pyramid or ziggurat. The base of this tower he measured as being 288 feet, and he estimated that it had been equally as high. Koldewey felt certain that this was the Biblical Tower of Babel. Constructed of an estimated 58,000,000 bricks and topped by a temple dedicated to Marduk, it must have dominated the Babylonian scene and impressed all observers.

The Tower of Babel was but one of many so-called legends that turned out to have a basis in fact. Woolley, in the course of his excavations, discovered signs of a tremendous flood, undoubtedly related to the Biblical Deluge. The more work progressed in Mesopotamian archaeology, the more legends came to life, though often in somewhat altered form. And it all began with the attempts to read bird tracks in the sand. The story of cuneiform scholarship is one of the great romances of archaeology, partly because it is a success story, but also because of its dramatic and colorful figures. For all the patient, uncolorful scholars who contributed so much to the story, we tend to remember Grotefend and his bet, or Rawlinson swinging down the face of a mountain, or Layard pursuing his boyhood dreams. That is the romance of archaeology.

Chapter Twelve

Sons of Heth and Canaanites

I

The once-mighty Egyptian civilization left its record behind in temples, pyramids, statues, and obelisks that fascinated centuries of travelers. The powerful ancient cities of the Near East, though buried and sometimes "lost," were still known by name and in legend. Perhaps the most fascinating discovery made by the nineteenth-century archaeologists was the most unexpected—that of a powerful and unknown empire that once had rivaled Egypt and Babylon. Though the Hittites had been known by name, their former greatness came as a surprise.

These people, so completely wiped from men's memories, came out of the mountains of Asia Minor about 2000 B.C., subdued the people of Hatti and took on their name, and grew in power. Under what we now call their Old Kingdom, they conquered Babylon but fell to the neighboring kingdom of Mitanni. Then a New Empire rose, subdued the Mitanni, as well as the Amorites

and Phoenicians, and took its place as one of the powerful nations of western Asia.

Much of the record of the Hittites is found not in
native chronicles, but in Egyptian accounts. There the
country is called *Ht,* which has been translated several
ways, Kheta being a common English rendering. A major
source of information about the Hittites is the Tell el
Amarna letters, official correspondence in cuneiform,
mostly Akkadian, which was the language of diplomacy
at one time. These letters between the rulers of Egypt
and those of Babylonia, Assyria, and Mitanni, discovered by accident in 1887, tell much of the story of the
waning of the Hittite Empire. We also have records
showing that Syria was called Land of the Hatti as
late as 717 B.C., when Sargon II captured Carchemish,
its eastern capital. After that the Hittites simply disap-
pear from all historical accounts.

They reappear, without being recognized, more than
2,500 years later in a most offhand and accidental way.
That story begins with Johann Ludwig Burckhardt, a
Swiss traveler and explorer. While in Hama, the Biblical Hamath, in 1812, Burckhardt noticed a stone with
strange hieroglyphics on it. The characters, he noted,
were different from Egyptian hieroglyphics, and he described the stone in a book which was published after
his death. Burckhardt did not consider his discovery
important, and because it failed to interest him further,
the Hittites were to remain in oblivion a bit longer.

Burckhardt's stone and some others like it in Hama,
which were also seen by the famous traveler Sir Richard

132

Burton, were rediscovered in the 1870's by two Americans. When they tried to make copies of the stones, five in all, the natives, who attributed curative powers to the stones, refused to let them be copied and even threatened to destroy them. Finally, the governor of Syria came with an Irish missionary, William Wright, to see the stones. With the help of the governor, casts were made of the stones and sent to the British Museum.

The strange writing on the Hama stones soon turned up in other parts of Asia Minor. William Wright contended that this script was the writing of the Hittìm (Hittites), mentioned in ancient Hebrew writings and appearing as the sons of Heth or children of Heth in the Old Testament. It was assumed that the Hittites were Semitic, but this assumption was soon challenged. In the Tell el Amarna letters there were two, addressed to the King of Arzawa, on the Mediterranean, written in an unknown language, fragments of which were also found near Bogazköy. The Norwegian J. A. Knudzton, studying this language in 1902, announced that it appeared to have Indo-European characteristics, a suggestion so ridiculed at the time that he withdrew it. The language, which proved to be that of the Hittites, is now generally recognized as Indo-European, the family of languages that includes English, most of the languages spoken in Europe, and several of southwestern Asia and India.

Hugo Winckler, the famous German archaeologist, headed expeditions to Bogazköy in 1906–7 and 1911–12 which uncovered more than 10,000 cuneiform tablets, some in Akkadian but most of them in the unknown

Arzawa language. Study of the Akkadian documents revealed that what had been uncovered was the official archives of the Hittite kingdom and that Bogazköy was the site of its ancient capital. Winckler transferred his findings to museums in Berlin and Constantinople shortly before World War I, making them available to scholars. But one thing was clear even without further study— the Kheta of the Egyptians, Hatti of the Babylonians and Hittim of the Hebrews were one and the same. The Hittites had reentered history.

II

Deciphering the language of the Hittites was a truly international affair. One of the earliest Hittite scholars was a Welshman. Archibald Henry Sayce, a professor of Assyriology at Oxford, was a born linguist who had read Latin and Greek at the age of ten and went on to master Hebrew, Egyptian, Persian and Sanskrit by the time he was eighteen. Sayce was given the task of studying some inscriptions found in northern Syria at a mound explored by George Smith on his last trip to the Near East. He concluded that the inscriptions were Hittite, the same as on the Hama stones, but he was more interested in the sculptures that had been dug up with them. These sculptures he found to be similar to others found elsewhere in Syria and Asia Minor. Sayce was so impressed by them that he felt that the Hittites had actually once been a great empire and not an insignificant tribe.

Then, in 1880, he recalled a silver plaque found by German diggers and written about in learned journals. This plaque had been discovered by A. D. Mordtmann, who wrote about it in 1863 calling it the Tarkondemos Boss. The term "boss" refers to a raised ornamentation on a flat disk, and this object was a thin silver plaque, or seal, about an inch and a half in diameter, containing pictures and writing. The round seal was divided by a concentric circle. Inside the circle was the figure of a warrior surrounded by various symbols; outside it was a cuneiform inscription, running around the circle like a border. The symbols ▲ ▲ and ▲ occurring inside the circle were also found at Hama, and Sayce identified them as country and king. In thus opening the way to the decipherment of the Hittite language, Sayce also concluded that it definitely was not Semitic.

Sayce read the seal inscription as "Tariktimme, King of the land of Erme"; today we read it as "Tarkumuwa, King of the land of Mera." But despite his incorrect translation, Sayce contributed one important point. He had recognized the symbols inside the circle as being Hittite and believed they should correspond to the cuneiform border inscription. In other words, the seal was bilingual, a miniature Hittite Rosetta Stone. Unfortunately, the Tarkondemos Boss contained only 6 hieroglyphs out of a known 200 symbols, not much to work with.

One consistent point being made was that the Hittite

language was not Semitic. The proof of this contention was provided by a Czech scholar. Bedřich Hrozný was born in Bohemia in 1879 and started studying ancient Oriental languages while he was a theology student. At the age of eighteen he switched to the study of languages and was so successful that in six years he became a professor at the University of Vienna. He began studying the Hittite language after Winckler's death in 1913, as one of many scholars working on that great archaeologist's findings at Bogazköy. Hrozný soon concluded that the language was Indo-European and succeeded in deciphering it by 1916. World War I had already started, and his sensational reports were published while he was serving in the army.

Hrozný was aided in his deciphering by the fact that Babylonian word-signs appeared in some of the Bogazköy texts. One phrase in particular led him to success, a phrase containing the word *ninda,* Babylonian for bread. It ran as follows:

nu NINDA-an ezzateni, vadar-ma ekuteni
(nu BREAD-an ezzateni, vadar-ma ekuteni)

which he worked out as "Now you will eat bread; then you will drink water." His reasoning was that the word "bread" should be accompanied by the expression "to eat"; the *ezza* of *ezzateni* suggested to eat. In line with this reasoning, *vadar* suggested water, and water is for drinking, just as bread is for eating. The word endings

136

he decided were expressions of case and tense; the same *teni* ending meant that eat and drink were of the same tense. Study of other inscriptions suggested "you will eat . . . you will drink" as the proper form.

If his theory was correct, the relationship of Hittite and modern languages was clear. Just compare *nu* in Hittite, *nun* in German, and "now" in English; or *vadar* in Hittite, *Wasser* in German and "water" in English; or *ezza, essen* and "to eat" in those languages. Though Hrozný went overboard in making such comparisons, other relationships with Indo-European were soon found in the Hittite language. Another ten years of study by various scholars proved Hrozný basically correct.

III

Slowly, and with the help of an increasingly international array of scholars, the study of the Hittite language progressed. By 1936, when E. H. Sturtevant published a glossary of more than 3,000 Hittite words and their meanings, certain basic facts had emerged. For one thing, it was determined that the language was read boustrophedon fashion (plow-wise), right to left and then left to right. For another, it was found that there were two styles of writing: monumental, which was elaborately carved in raised relief, and cursive, which

was simplified and incised. The hieroglyph in the

monumental form was matched by the cursive ⋂ , or

the monumental ▢▯▢ had the cursive ∘ʃ∘ as its

counterpart.

Few examples of the cursive writing have survived compared to the monumental. The Hittites wrote with brush and ink on tablets of wood backed with white-washed linen. Official documents were engraved on silver, iron, or lead, but the main writing material was wood, which has not survived the centuries. The monumental inscriptions were usually chiseled in stone, which indicates they were probably first incised in some less permanent material and then copied.

We also know that the Hittites used cuneiform for daily purposes and their hieroglyphics for monumental purposes. They were thus bilingual, using Akkadian and Hittite. The cuneiform, acquired from the Babylonians, could be read and understood by the early scholars when it was in Akkadian and read but not understood when it was in Hittite. The hieroglyphic writing, which was not Egyptian but may have been inspired by it, could not be read or understood by the early scholars. But in one sense the hieroglyphs were recognizable. They were identifiable representations of parts of the body, animal heads, and even pieces of furniture. How to read them was still a matter of guesswork ten years after Hrozný's findings. Some scholars felt that, in the absence of an extensive bilingual key, the prospect for deciphering them seemed hopeless. Five scholars from five countries felt otherwise.

One of the five was the Czech Bedřich Hrozný. Another was the Italian Piero Meriggi. A linguist of international fame, Meriggi not only helped decipher the Hittite hieroglyphic writing, but also advanced the study of other ancient languages—Lycian, Lydian, Luvian, the Indus script, and Creto-Mycenaean. The third was the American I. J. Gelb, a professor at the Oriental Institute of the University of Chicago. One of his important contributions was to sum up the work of his colleagues and predecessors in *Hittite Hieroglyphs,* published in three volumes in 1931, 1935, and 1942.

Gelb worked out various phonetic values from place-names, using Assyrian renderings of Hittite names. He also determined that the hieroglyphs were both ideograms and phonograms. Gelb concluded that the Hittite language contained about sixty phonetic signs, too many for the writing to be alphabetic. He further concluded that no signs began with a vowel, but that all ended with one, and that there were no closed syllables. In other words, there was not *ap,* but *pa,* and no *pam.* A closed syllable was written by using two syllables ending in a vowel; thus, instead of *pam,* there was *pa* plus *me.*

Further advances were made by the Swiss scholar Emil Forrer, who found eight different languages used in the tablets uncovered at Bogazköy. Forrer was opposed to a straight phonetic reading of the Hittite characters. He pointed out that Chinese ideograms are read in Japanese

139

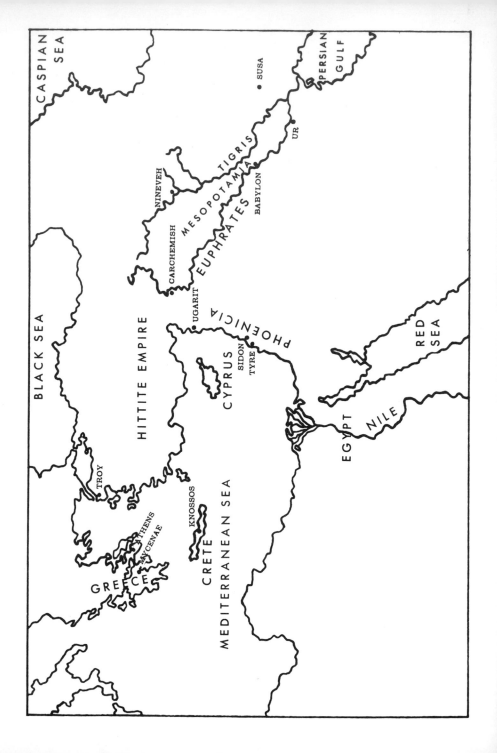

in Japan or in Korean in Korea. In the same way, he felt, Sumerian ideograms were pronounced in Assyrian in Assyria and in Hittite in the kingdom of the Hittites. Forrer revealed the grammatical structure of the hieroglyphic language, pointed out various parallels in the structure and writing of different languages, and also noted similarities throughout the ancient East of initial formulas at the openings of royal inscriptions, formulas of curses, and opening phrases of letters.

The fifth scholar to advance the study of Hittite hieroglyphics, the German Helmuth Theodor Bossert, started out as an art historian. His interest in archaeology and paleography led him to devote the years 1929 to 1931 to the study of Minoan writing. In the summer of 1933 he went to Turkey to collect rock inscriptions. While there, he was invited to Bogazköy and began his study of the Hittite inscriptions. World War II put a stop to most archaeological excavations, but Bossert was digging in the foothills of the Taurus Mountains a year afterward. In 1947, working mainly at Kara Tepe (Black Mountain), he found two companion slabs, one inscribed in Old Phoenician, the other in Hittite hieroglyphics. These slabs confirmed theories about Hittite grammar and writing and have extended the known vocabulary.

Among the texts found at Bogazköy are copies of the Gilgamesh Epic in several languages, including Akkadian and Hittite, as well as other local epics. There are also rituals, edicts, directives, and a body of laws inspired by the Code of Hammurabi. All these must be

141

studied for what new information they may yield. The work is far from over. By 1949 the five great Hittologists had established an agreed-on list of phonetic values, but their work, too, is not finished. Many questions and problems remain, and the Hittite language is still largely unintelligible.

IV

One of the companion tablets Bossert found at Kara Tepe contained Hittite hieroglyphics; the other was inscribed with Old Phoenician characters. This discovery may have been more inspiring than it was helpful. For the Phoenician language represents that rare example: an unknown tongue in an unknown script deciphered without a bilingual text.

The Phoenicians were a seafaring people living along the eastern shore of the Mediterranean Sea. They built a great commercial empire, more than 3,000 years ago, partly on the fame of their purple dye, but mostly on the strength of their seamanship. Phoenician sailors early crossed the Mediterranean, founding what is now Cádiz, in Spain, and visiting the British coast. Their greatest accomplishment, undertaken about 600 B.C. at the order of an Egyptian pharaoh, was the circumnavigation of Africa. They also spread their culture in their travels, and it is from them that the Greeks received the Semitic script, either in the form of a consonantal alphabet or as a syllabary without vowels.

Until early in the twentieth century, the oldest known

sample of Phoenician writing was the Moabite Stone, a thirty-four line inscription dating from about 850 B.C. More recent discoveries have taken this writing back several centuries and indicate that the Canaanites, the original settlers of Phoenicia, were experimenting with various forms of writing, including cuneiform, from about 1500 B.C. The area settled by the Canaanites was open to many influences. Egyptian records tell of sea expeditions to their coast as early as about 2650 B.C., and later records tell of the rise of the famous coastal cities of Tyre, Sidon, and Acco (Acre). In Homeric times Sidon was so famous that the Phoenicians were called Sidonians. Of the many Phoenician cities identifiable from ancient accounts, one of them, Ugarit, somehow remained unknown and undiscovered for centuries. Its mystery, in fact, was solved by accident.

A few miles north of Latakia (ancient Laodicea), on the Syrian coast opposite Cyprus, is Minet el-Beida (White Harbor). On April 25, 1928, a native plowing a field there discovered an underground passage leading to a burial chamber. Word of the find reached the governor, who informed the Bureau of Antiquities in Beirut. Soon information was being circulated and, when the plans of the sepulcher reached Paris, René Dussaud saw its close resemblance to the vaulted tombs of Mycenae. Meanwhile, Aegean pottery fragments had been found at the site that dated from the second millennium B.C. Clearly further expert study was called for, and the Institut de France sent an archaeological expedition to White Harbor.

Excavations began in 1929 in the vicinity of the burial chamber and then at the nearby mound of Ras Shamra (Cape Fennel or Fennel Head), a sixty-foot hill overgrown with aromatic fennel. Ras Shamra was a towering deposit of man-made debris that turned out to be the long-lost Ugarit. Egyptian and Hittite relics were found at the site, and Ugarit's history was pieced together back to the Neolithic period, in the fifth millennium B.C. The arrival of the Canaanites was put at somewhere between 3000 and 2000 B.C., and it was established that the city was destroyed and lost to history in the twelfth century B.C., when the region was overrun by the Assyrians.

Shortly after the digging began, samples of the long-missing Canaanite literature were uncovered on clay tablets inscribed in cuneiform, some of them Akkadian but most in an unknown writing. The writing was thought to be alphabetic, because it contained about thirty cuneiform characters. It was studied by French and German Semitic scholars, who concluded it was a Semitic dialect, probably Canaanite (Phoenician).

The Frenchman Charles Virolleaud, who had visited the burial chamber that was the first Canaanite discovery, decided that some of the tablets contained correspondence, which he read as beginning "To (so-and-so)." He identified "to" with the Semitic *l* and searched for words containing an *l*. Soon he found *mlk*, which corresponded to the Hebrew word for king. Proceeding quickly from this start, he worked out translations of various numbers and such words as vine, olive, cedar,

144

judge, and throne. Meanwhile, other scholars, chiefly the German Hans Bauer and the Frenchman Édouard Dhorme, worked on other texts. In the remarkably short time of a few months they solved the problem of deciphering the Ugaritic language and writing. Bauer accomplished some of the most basic work in the amazing time of one week.

Twenty years later, excavations at Ras Shamra turned up a small tablet that provided a complete ABC of the cuneiform script. Other excavations turned up dictionaries for school use, legal documents, a horse-training manual, and price lists of goods sold in the bazaar. But most of the findings were mythological and religious works, the most interesting of which is known as the Legend of Keret. Study of this and other works led to two theories: one that Ugaritic is a distinct language related to Akkadian and Canaanite, and the other that Ugaritic and Hebrew are West Semitic dialects that may be called Canaanite.

Comparison of Ugaritic and Hebrew revealed similarities that can be explained only by some very close relationship. Both writings show similar features of style, and both refer to the same specific things, such as the monster leviathan. Ugaritic references to Canaanite religious practices read like ritual practices in the Old Testament and even contain familiar Biblical phraseology. Presumably much of the lost Canaanite writing had been preserved all along in the sacred writings of their Hebrew conquerors.

Chapter Thirteen

Land of the Minotaur

I

There are two histories of Crete, the real one, compiled by the archaeologists, and the legendary one, left to us by the ancient Greeks. The legend is one of the most fascinating tales ever told and is still the subject of modern fiction. The true history is also fascinating, partly because it supports the legend, but also because it reveals the existence of a rich, powerful, and cultured civilization that flourished and died more than 3,000 years ago.

Crete is a large island in the Mediterranean Sea, situated just south of the Greek mainland and the Aegean Sea. It is marked by rocky coasts and a mountainous interior, capped by Mount Ida in its center, more than 8,000 feet high. The early settlers of Crete arrived between 4000 and 3000 B.C., probably from Anatolia and Syria. Evidence indicates that they were influenced by the Egyptian and Lybian civilizations south of them across the Mediterranean. From these origins and influences grew the Minoan civilization that made Crete a power in the ancient world.

The Early Minoan Period (2800–1800 B.C.) was a time when towns were being built up and when metalwork was still poor. The Middle Minoan Period (1800–1600 B.C.) saw the rise to power of Knossos, the principal Cretan city, and the building of great palaces. This period is marked by improved potterywork, by metalwork in bronze, and by the building up of Crete's naval power and overseas trade.

In the Late Minoan Period (1550–1100 B.C.) Crete was a world power along with Egypt and the Hittite Empire. Then Knossos was the hub of a centralized government that ruled the island and an overseas empire. About 1400 B.C. Knossos was destroyed, either by an invasion, which ties in with the legend, or by an earthquake. After the fall of Knossos, mainland cities like Mycenae rose to power; the remains of Cretan civilization survived Knossos for a while, but what remained was gradually absorbed into the general Aegean civilization.

According to tradition, Zeus, the chief of gods, either was born on Crete, in a cave on the southern part of the island, or was taken to such a cave after having been born elsewhere. Tradition also states that Minos, King of Crete, was a son of Zeus. The powerful Minos was a lawgiver and founder of the first great naval power in the Mediterranean. He was also overlord of Athens and, as such,

147

demanded a yearly tribute of twelve noble Athenian youths and maidens to sacrifice to the Minotaur. This monster, half man and half bull, was kept beneath the palace of Minos in a maze called the labyrinth. This maze, designed by Daedalus, had so many twisting passages that no one could find his way out of it, and everyone would wander helplessly until he reached the center where the Minotaur was waiting to slay him.

One year, according to the legend, Theseus, son of Aegeus, the lord of Athens, went to Crete as one of the victims. There Ariadne, Minos' daughter, fell in love with him and agreed to help him. Ariadne gave Theseus a thread to mark his trail through the labyrinth. Entering the maze, Theseus found and slew the Minotaur, then escaped by following the thread back out. He destroyed Minos' palace and fled with Ariadne, who left him at an island called Naxos. Meanwhile, Minos imprisoned Daedalus for helping Ariadne, locking him up in a tower with his son, Icarus. Daedalus fashioned wings of wax and feathers to escape with, but Icarus flew too high, and the sun melted his wings. Minos pursued Daedalus, who had escaped successfully but was killed mysteriously before he could capture the maze-maker.

So goes the legend. We cannot be certain what the Minotaur was or if there was a real Theseus. But visitors to Crete can see the maze that existed beneath the palace at Knossos, and the bull dancers in Minoan wall paintings seem to be engaged in some ritual.

II

After you discover Troy and Mycenae, what do you do for an encore? Heinrich Schliemann turned to Crete. In 1883 the famous excavator of Troy and Mycenae applied to the Turkish government, then rulers of Crete, for permission to dig there. Three years later, at the age of sixty-four, he arrived at the mound of Kephala, the traditional site of Knossos. Spanish diggers at Kephala in 1877 had established the existence, at a very great depth, of a building measuring 180 feet by 140 feet. Schliemann could not conclude satisfactory negotiations to buy the site and eventually gave up his plans to dig there. In 1894, however, a young man who had met Schliemann and who had been impressed by him and inspired by his discoveries made his first visit to Crete. This was Arthur Evans, with whose name Cretan archaeology is forever bound.

Arthur Evans was born in 1851 into a scholarly and well-to-do Victorian family. Extremely nearsighted and not inclined toward sports, Evans was nevertheless an adventurous young man who loved travel and undertook many dangerous journeys. He traveled repeatedly in the Balkans, at times as a journalist, all the while pursuing two hobbies—archaeology and the study of old coins.

In 1878 Evans became engaged to Margaret Freeman. The couple celebrated the occasion by visiting the exhibition of Trojan antiquities that had been brought to

149

London by Heinrich Schliemann. In the early 1880's Evans and his wife visited Greece. There they met the Schliemanns at their home and then went to Tiryns and Mycenae, where Schliemann had excavated. In 1884, back in England, Evans became curator of the Ashmolean Museum, a position which allowed him to continue with his travels. This he did, though his wife died in 1893, while the couple was on a Mediterranean journey.

That year, while in Athens, Evans found at an antiquity dealer's small three- and four-sided stones, drilled along the axis and engraved with symbols that seemed to be hieroglyphic in nature. Conditioned by his nearsightedness to examine small objects close up, Evans studied these stones and various seals and signet rings, which, he learned, had come from Crete. In 1894 he visited the site of Knossos, hoping to find more "pictographs," as he called the hieroglyphics, but he did not begin digging there until five years later, when Turkish rule of the island ended. In the intervening years he visited and observed, finding many ornamental stones which Cretan women had worn since ancient times, all with the intriguing hieroglyphics.

When digging began in March, 1899, Evans and the experienced excavators who were his associates soon found a great labyrinth of buildings at the mound of Kephala. Evans was convinced that the civilization he had uncovered was pre-Mycenaean, but his principal interest was in discovering more samples of the mysterious writing and in deciphering it. Though he did manage to dig up hundreds of samples, he could not ignore the greater importance of having uncovered a pre-Homeric civilization of an apparently high order, stretching Aegean history back several centuries.

Evans and his party discovered a wall fresco that included part of a life-size figure, the first look any modern observer had of a Cretan inhabitant of 1500 B.C. An excited Evans wrote: ". . . it is far and away the most remarkable human figure of the Mycenaean age that has yet come to light." He called the people Minoan, after the legendary King Minos, and continued excavating. More and more of the vast structure was revealed— storerooms, an administrative center, and a throne room. Evans was fascinated by his discoveries of frescoes and seals depicting bulls, for the Theseus legend was always in his mind. Then he uncovered a fresco that showed a young man somersaulting over a bull and a girl in costume waiting to catch him. Soon other examples of this scene showed up. Were these bull leapers hostages sent to be sacrificed to the Minotaur?

To Evans the civilization at Knossos clearly seemed akin to that of Mycenae; it also seemed to be much older. The obvious deduction from this is that the Mycenaean civilization must have come from Crete. Evans dug up evidence that Knossos had been settled from at least 3000 B.C. to at least 1200 B.C. In addition to dating Cretan civilization back to Neolithic times, Evans found evidence that Minoan Crete had indeed been the world's first naval power. More of the legend was being proved true. At the same time, D. G. Hogarth, director of the British School of Archaeology in Athens, was digging at the sacred cave that was the legendary birth-place of Zeus. Hogarth found knives, double axes, orna-ments, and convincing indications that the cave was a specially sacred grotto and a sanctuary of Zeus. Here certainly was the birth cave of Zeus, just as the legend said.

III

For better or worse, Evans' long work at Crete bears the definite stamp of his personal ideas and inclinations. Despite the competence of his associates, he was very soon determined to excavate in his own way. "I must have sole control of what I am personally undertaking," he wrote his father. And, over the years, his father and then Evans himself spent probably 250,000 pounds of the family fortune carrying out the excavations Evans' way. This does not mean he worked out of touch with the world of archaeology. In 1901, for instance, he took time off to visit his friend Federigo Halbherr, the Italian archaeologist who was excavating another Minoan pal-ace at Phaistos in the south of Crete.

His work and views, however, remained highly per-sonal. When he uncovered and restored a magnificent staircase and the main hall of the palace at Knossos, he began a quarrel with Hogarth about his reconstructions. These extravagant re-creations, said Hogarth, were more suited for impressing spectators than for true archaeological purposes. For the next thirty years, however, Evans devoted his time and money to excavating and reconstructing the palace of Minos in his own way. He wrote about his work in *The Palace of Minos* but, true to form, published his findings as he saw fit. His delay in publishing some findings, such as all the examples of writing he had uncovered, hampered the work of other scholars. The simple fact is that though other archaeologists uncovered Minoan sites in Crete, Evans had the finest site for himself and enough money to excavate and restore it just as he wished. Archaeologists and scholars since Hogarth's time have questioned the accuracy of some of the details of Evans' restored palace rooms. Some of his interpretations of Cretan history have been disproved, and most contemporary scholars disagree with his contention that the palace of Minos was destroyed by an earthquake. Nevertheless, we are greatly indebted to him for all the work he did at Crete.

The problem of the Cretan writing dogged him throughout his long career. Evans decided, correctly, that the clay tablets with writing he had unearthed were inventories. "It appears," he wrote perhaps sadly, "that the documents in an overwhelming degree refer to accounts and lists of persons and possessions." Though he managed to decipher numerals, Evans was disappointed with this limited success. For he never managed to decipher the mysterious Minoan script, and it was this which had brought him to Crete in the first place.

153

IV

The Minoans maintained cultural and commercial contacts with the Egyptians from earliest times, and it is through Egyptian objects found in Crete that archaeologists have worked out Cretan dating. When Evans found an Egyptian statue of the twelfth dynasty (2000–1700 B.C.) embedded in one of the strata of his dig at the palace of Knossos, he could reasonably assume that the date of that stratum was approximately 2000 B.C. Egyptian objects have been found at various sites in Crete along with Minoan pottery and other objects. It is, therefore, equally reasonable to assume that if Egyptian objects of a particular dynasty are always found with Cretan objects, wall paintings, or architecture of a certain kind, then all Minoan pottery, wall paintings, or architecture of that kind can be given a rough date. In this way, some objects found in Crete have been dated back to predynastic times, before 3200 B.C. Minoan objects and artwork, it should also be noted, show up in Egypt, as well as throughout the Aegean area and in mainland Greece. Some of these provide further clues to Cretan history.

Evans divided the Minoan civilization into three great periods which he related to the three great Egyptian periods of Old Kingdom, Middle Empire, and New Empire. Through the comparison method it became possible to date not only Cretan findings, but also discoveries at Troy, Mycenae, and elsewhere. Mycenaean

154

treasures dated at about 1600 B.C., predating the Trojan War, could not have belonged to Agamemnon, the Mycenaean general in the war. Yet these treasures were, to Evans, representative of Late Minoan culture; 1600 B.C. was only 200 years before the destruction of Knossos. Thus, it seemed perfectly clear to Evans that the Cretan civilization was older than the Mycenaean.

Year after year Evans worked at reconstructing the palace, turning to the use of reinforced concrete when he found that wood rotted too quickly and brickwork or masonry was too expensive. As the work progressed, his discoveries revealed much of the ancient religious practices, which he linked to earth worship. He found many representations of a goddess whom he called the Minoan mother goddess and roughly dated various disasters he felt had been due to earthquakes. His excavations and reconstructions of private chambers also revealed much of daily life in ancient Crete. One of his most fascinating discoveries was of the remarkable plumbing facilities and hydraulic engineering of these ancient people.

In 1908, Evans gave up the keepership of the Ashmolean in order to devote more time to his work in Crete. He retained the honorary post of visitor to the Ashmolean, however, keeping an eye on its affairs and continuing to shower it with gifts throughout his life. In 1911, at the age of sixty, he was knighted for his overall contribution to learning. Ten years later, before returning to Crete after a halt in work during World War

I, he finally published the first volume of *The Palace of Minos*. The book would eventually run to several volumes, more than 3,000 pages in length, with 2,400 illustrations, many in color.

While excavating in Crete in 1926, he experienced what he considered a dramatic proof of his theories. On a June evening, while he was lying in bed reading, an earthquake struck the area. The walls of his house trembled; his bed rocked; objects tumbled all around him. "A dull sound rose from the ground like the muffled roar of an angry bull," he later wrote. Though his reconstruction, bolstered throughout by steel pillars, withstood the shock, the surrounding area for miles around was devastated. The experience confirmed his belief in an earthquake as the destructive force at Knossos and in earth worship as the basis of religion in ancient Crete.

Evans continued excavating at the advanced age of eighty and died shortly after his ninetieth birthday. This was during World War II and at a sad time for the old man, for his beloved Crete, Greece, and the Balkans had been invaded by the Nazis. He had visited Crete for the last time at the age of eighty-eight when he had gone to receive honors there. At the ceremonies he made a statement that sums up one of the main points of Cretan archaeology. "We know now," said Evans, "that the old traditions were true."

Chapter Fourteen

Ventris and Linear B

I

The mysterious hieroglyphics, neither Egyptian nor Babylonian, had brought Arthur Evans to Crete, but nearly half a century of studying them had left him far from solving their riddle. The solution was provided less than fifteen years after Evans' death by a young man who had not spent a lifetime excavating in Crete, who was not even an archaeologist, and whose efforts were performed strictly as an amateur. Perhaps ironically, it was Evans who inspired Michael Ventris, the decipherer of the Minoan writing, to pursue this intriguing puzzle.

Evans had noted three stages of writing in Crete. The earliest form, in use from about 2000 to 1650 B.C., he called hieroglyphic. This writing, the same as he had found on the seal stones that first attracted his attention, was made up of pictorial signs representing a head, a hand, a star, an arrow, and other such objects. In the next, more cursive form, the pictures were reduced to outlines. This stage of writing, in use from about 1750 to 1450 B.C., he called Linear A. He noted also that it was written from left to right and was found only in Crete. At some undetermined date, said Evans, this writing was replaced by what he called Linear B, a modification in use at the time of the destruction of Knossos (1400 B.C.).

Linear B was not a simpler form of Linear A; Evans could not fail to notice that it was at times more elaborate. He thought that this "royal" writing was used only at Knossos, but samples have been found in mainland Greece. The current explanation that Linear B was an adaptation of the Minoan script used for writing Greek is only a partial explanation of the script's development and use. Scholars have noted that Linear A and Linear B are superficially alike, but the differences between them, even more noticeable, remain part of the mystery of Linear A.

One of the first things that had to be determined about Linear B was whether it was ideographic, syllabic, or alphabetic. An ideographic script, like Chinese, uses many thousands of ideograms. A syllabic system, while using far fewer signs, nevertheless employs a high number of them. Alphabetic writing, which was invented by the Semites and developed by the Greeks, uses a small number of signs. There are, for instance, twenty-six letters in our alphabet, or thirty-two in the more complicated Russian one.

Early study of Linear B demonstrated that some signs, standing alone and followed by a numeral, were definitely ideographic. When the signs appear in groups, there seemed to be about eighty-nine of them, though the exact number is disputed—too many for an alphabetic script and too few for an ideographic script. The obvious conclusion was that Linear B probably employed a simple syllabary, like Cypriot or Japanese. It was Evans who had supplied an important clue by working out the system of numbers used in the writing. He found that a vertical stroke stood for 1; a horizontal stroke for 10; a circle for 100; a circle with lines or rays at the cardinal points for 1,000; and the same with a horizontal bar in the center for 10,000.

Another clue available to early scholars of the Minoan script was an object known as the Phaistos Disk. Found in 1908 by the Italian excavator Luigi Pernier at the Minoan palace at Phaistos in southern Crete, it is a flat disk of baked clay, six and a half inches in diameter, inscribed on both sides with a text running spirally from rim to center. The inscriptions contain a total of 241 pictorial signs—people, animals, houses, etc.—arranged in groups or sections of from 2 to 5 signs each. There are 118 signs in thirty sections on one face of the disk and 123 signs in thirty-one sections on the other. Because the figures faced right, Pernier concluded that the inscriptions should be read right to left, thus from the outside of the spiral inward to the center. He also recognized 45 different pictorial signs, which he arranged in seven groupings, such as Vegetation and Plants or Arms and Tools.

The most remarkable feature of the Phaistos Disk is that it was not "written." Each sign was impressed on the soft clay by a punch, more or less an early form of printing. Though it seems most unlikely that a set of forty-five punches was made just to prepare this disk, the fact remains that no other such disk has ever been discovered. As for the language of the disk, it bears some resemblance to Cretan hieroglyphics but remains undeciphered. A clue to the Minoan script it seems to be, but a puzzling one at best.

Still another early clue was the Cypriot script, used for the writing of Greek from the sixth to the third or second centuries B.C. The key to its decipherment was discovered by George Smith, of Gilgamesh fame, in the 1870's. The Cypriot script is clearly related to Linear B; seven signs are easily equated, and others display some resemblances. But even where the Cypriot script seemed to promise the most clear-cut help in deciphering the Cretan writing, it created problems for the scholars.

A high proportion of Cypriot words end in *se,* and the most common final consonant in Greek is *s.* The *se* sign in Cypriot is matched by a similar sign in

Linear B. But this sign rarely appears as a word ending in Linear B, suggesting that Linear B is not a form of Greek. Students of writing, however, know that the same sign in related languages can stand for different sounds. Some scholars were not convinced, as Evans

was, that the 𝗟𝗟𝗟 sign proved that Linear B was not

a form of Greek. Moreover, other discoveries did indicate a relationship to Greek. Once again the clues promised more than they delivered. Linear B was at a stage of decipherment comparable to hieroglyphics in the hands of Thomas Young. It was waiting for its Champollion to solve the puzzle, and he arrived in the person of Michael Ventris.

II

Michael Ventris was born on July 12, 1922, into a well-to-do English family. He was schooled in Switzerland, where he learned French and German and spoke the local Swiss-German dialect. A natural linguist, he later taught himself Polish and Swedish. During World War II he was a navigator in the Royal Air Force (RAF), which he found "so much more interesting than mere flying." After the war he returned to his study of architecture, which remained his actual occupation for the remainder of his short life.

Ventris' interest in ancient languages dated back to

when he was a boy of seven, spurred by his reading of a German book on Egyptian hieroglyphics. He became interested in Crete at the age of fourteen, when he visited Burlington House in London to see an exhibition honoring the fiftieth anniversary of the British School of Archaeology in Athens. At this exhibition young Ventris attended a lecture by Arthur Evans and was inspired to study the mysterious script that so fascinated the great archaeologist. Before he was twenty, Ventris was a serious student of Cretan writing and, though he remained an amateur, shared ideas with scholars throughout the world.

When Ventris began his serious study of the Cretan writing, the available clues not only were unrevealing, but were also few in number. There were no trilingual texts like the Rosetta Stone or the Rock of Behistun to work from. There were no bilingual clues either, not even Greek ones, and the symbols bore no relation to modern forms of writing. But this did not deter Ventris. As he later explained in an article for *Antiquity* magazine, he planned his deciphering in three phases: (1) "an exhaustive analysis of the signs, words and contexts"—which meant studying every available inscription and looking for every clue to spelling, meaning and structure; (2) "an experimental substitution of phonetic values"—which could hopefully reveal possible words in a known language; and (3) "a decisive check"—which, particularly with fresh material, would ensure that the results are not due to coincidence or some mistake.

To accomplish "an exhaustive analysis of the signs, words and contexts" requires sufficient samples to work from. When Ventris started, of the more than 2,800 tablets and fragments uncovered in Crete, only 142 had been published. In 1939 American excavators at Pylos, on the Greek mainland, uncovered 600 tablets written in Linear B. These inscriptions, which showed that the script was still in use on the mainland 200 years after the destruction of Knossos, were published in 1951. A year later one of Evans' associates finally published his unfinished second volume of *Scripta Minoa,* making available all the Linear B tablets found at Knossos. A truly "exhaustive" analysis was not possible, therefore, until the early 1950's.

Despite the shortage of inscriptions to work from, by 1940, when Ventris began his deciphering, it was generally agreed that the script contained about seventy signs for sound values, plus ideograms for men and women and such objects as chariots, horses, and swords. After World War II, study resumed at about this point, and in 1947 some studies were begun on the Pylos tablets. In 1950 Ventris polled the leading scholars about their thoughts on the relationship of Linear A to Linear B and what language they thought the Cretan writing would prove to be. He himself had for ten years thought of it as Etruscan, a form he called Aegean. Most of the scholars thought it would turn out to be an Indo-European language related to Hittite. No one suggested Greek.

For the next two years, despite his full-time job as

architect for the ministry of education and his repeated promises to put aside deciphering, Ventris worked at the puzzle of Linear B, circulating his work notes to the scholars in the field. Meanwhile, the publication of *The Pylos Tablets* made available accurate copies of many signs. Ventris, shifting his basic approach, began constructing the grid that became his basic working tool and began looking for place-names in configurations called triplets. The grid and the triplets, which require separate detailed discussion, provided the key to decipherment of Linear B.

Up to 1950 it had been generally assumed that Linear B was the script of a non-Greek language, like Linear A. Evans flatly stated that Linear B developed from Linear A. But in 1950 E. L. Bennett, the American scholar who was preparing the Pylos inscriptions for publication, pointed out signs in Linear B that looked the same as Greek signs, even though the words in which they appeared seemed different. Of course, any linguist was familiar with this situation; after all, English, French, and German all use the same letters. Linear B, therefore, could be an archaic form of Greek using Minoan symbols. When this possibility occurred to Ventris, he began to correspond with Bennett. During 1951 and 1952, when Bennett went to Crete to check on his recently published inscriptions, he continued to correspond with Ventris, who also kept in touch with other scholars. One of these scholars was Professor C. W. Blegen, who had made the actual discoveries at Pylos and who, in 1952, was back there. This time he discovered 400 more tablets, which he turned over to Bennett for publication.

In June, 1952, Ventris made a momentous announcement. The occasion was a radio talk on the BBC that he had been asked to make in connection with the publication of *Scripta Minoa II*. "During the last few weeks," said Ventris, "I have come to the conclusion that the Knossos and Pylos tablets must, after all, be written in Greek—a difficult and archaic Greek, seeing that is it 500 years older than Homer and written in a rather abbreviated form, but Greek nevertheless.

"Once I made this assumption, most of the peculiarities of the language and spelling which had puzzled me seemed to find a logical explanation, and although many of the tablets remain as incomprehensible as before, many others are suddenly beginning to make sense." He was saying that he had solved the puzzle of Linear B.

III

One result of Ventris' radio talk was that he began his association with John Chadwick, a Cambridge philologist. The book by Ventris and Chadwick, *Documents in Mycenaean Greek,* completed in 1955 and published shortly after Ventris' death, is the formal presentation of his theory and how it had been worked out. Ventris, following his three-phase plan, compiled lists of the frequency with which certain signs appeared—how many times at the beginning, in the middle, or at the end of a word. Next, he analyzed the apparent grammatical structure of the language, checking the interrelationships of the phonetic signs and the relative frequency of their appearance. Then he constructed a grid in which the vertical columns each contained a single vowel and the horizontal rows each contained a single consonant. At last he was ready for "a reasonably controlled experiment in allotting phonetic values."

The so-called grid was not original with Ventris. It grew out of the work of an American, Alice Kober, who kept up the studies of Linear B during World War II. Dr. Kober worked out what she called "the beginning of a tentative pattern," a grouping of the syllabic signs according to their presumed vowel and possible consonant content. Her pattern was arranged so that it could be extended in either direction:

	VOWEL 1	VOWEL 2	VOWEL 3	→
CONSONANT 1				
CONSONANT 2				
CONSONANT 3				
↓				

or to show it with examples:

	O	U	?
V	VO	VU	V?
C	CO	CU	C?
N	NO	NU	N?
?	?O	?U	??

166

The decoders turned her pattern into an actual grid. They set up a board with nails, used as pegs, on which could be hung the various syllabic signs. This allowed them to move the signs around as new discoveries were made.

Ventris began his experimentation with phonetic values by turning to a presumably promising source, the Cypriot syllabary. He examined previous attempts to assign the values in terms of Cypriot and tried his own hand at it, he said, because of its "supposed resemblances" to signs used in Linear B. After some intensive work he decided to give up the comparison, and the relation of the Cypriot syllabary and Linear B remains unproved. "It is clear," wrote Ventris, "that the values of the 'Linear B' signs must be fixed on internal evidence, and to satisfy the 'grid' and inflexions already found, without taking into account any other doubtfully related writing systems."

He pursued his study of Alice Kober's work, which had been done while he was a navigator with the RAF, noting her discovery of inflectional endings and a consistent series of words which, in different contexts, recurred in three different forms. Dr. Kober called these paradigms; Ventris called them triplets and thought they might be the names of the chief Cretan cities with corresponding adjectives. Dr. Kober thought the first sign of the first triplet was *A,* and Ventris agreed, because vowels are common in an initial position. "The decisive step," he said, "was to identify the first words with Amnissos, and to substitute values which would turn the others into Knossos, Tylissos, Phaestos, and Lyktos."

167

Soon he had tentatively assigned about fifty signs to places on his grid. Their positions would be fixed—that is, the decipherments he had substituted for the Linear B signs would be proved—only if his entire experiment worked. If the words he was then working with, for instance, were not the names he supposed, "then the resulting system of values must inevitably be a completely dislocated jumble." That no jumble resulted is a matter of history. In fact, when he applied his experimental phonetic values to the pattern of declensions he had analyzed, Ventris found that they "fell into line" with the known Greek system of declensions and specifically with its archaic forms.

Like Evans, Ventris had originally thought that the mysterious language was Minoan and not connected with Greek or any other known language. Only when he experimentally attributed Greek values to the signs did he realize that the language could be read as an archaic form of Greek. He deciphered such things as an inventory of swords, which included a pictogram of a sword and ended with a number and the phrase *to-sa pa-ka-na,* (so many swords). This phrase in Greek would be *tossa phasgana.* Other similarities showed up; a tablet with a pictogram of a chariot which describes the wheels as *kakodeta* (bound with bronze) or *kakia* (brazen), and names which, when deciphered, matched those of the Greek gods Zeus, Poseidon, Hera, and "Lady Athena."

Having accomplished step one, "exhaustive analysis," and step two, "experimental substitution," Ventris was

168

ready for step three, checking his results on "virgin material" to prove that his results were not due to coincidence or, as he put it, "fantasy." He turned to a tablet found at Pylos in 1952 containing drawings of tripods and vases. Reading the inscription on this tablet, he came up with *ti-ri-po-de,* the Greek word for tripods. In May, 1953, came welcome support for Ventris' theory. Professor Blegen wrote from Greece, where he was getting tablets from Pylos in proper shape to be photographed, to tell Ventris that he had "tried your experimental syllabary on some of them.

"Enclosed for your information," wrote Blegen, "is a copy of P641, which you may find interesting. It evidently deals with pots, some on three legs, some with four handles, some with three, and others without handles. The first word by your system seems to be ti-ri-po-de and it recurs twice as ti-ri-po (singular?). The four-handled pot is preceded by qe-to-ro-we, the three-handled by ti-ri-o-we or ti-ri-jo-we, the handless pot by a-no-we. All this seems too good to be true. Is coincidence excluded?"

IV

It is now generally accepted by scholars that the language of the Linear B tablets is an early form of Greek. The use of Minoan writing beyond the island of Crete, it is believed, resulted from control of the mainland by the government at Knossos during the period called Late Minoan II. It is further believed that the Mycenaean

Linear B script was derived from an earlier Minoan version, probably Linear A, which can be traced back to Cretan hieroglyphic writing. This hieroglyphic writing is noted as being Egyptian in character but is considered an independent system.

What happened to this developing language that the versatile and inventive Greeks seem to have abandoned? After the destruction of the centers of culture at the close of the Bronze Age, there is a gap of more than three centuries. Then when Greek writing reappears, it is in a Phoenician, rather than a Minoan, form. The distinguished scholar A. J. B. Wace has suggested that Linear B continued in use during the Iron Age, but was gradually abandoned in favor of the Phoenician system, which had obvious advantages to offer. Archaeological evidence from the little-known three centuries may someday prove this reasonable theory.

Another kind of gap hampers the study of Linear B. All the inscriptions that have been deciphered are mere inventories. However, Ventris' theory has been proved, and with the key he provided, future scholars will be able to translate any newly discovered inscriptions more interesting than inventories. No firsthand history has come down to us in Linear B, and no literature. There is only one mention of writing in Homer, in Book VI of the *Iliad;* it remains the one known literary reference to Minoan or Mycenaean writing.

But work on the Cretan tablets has only begun. Linear A is still a mystery to the scholars and may prove to be truly Minoan. A missing literature or a firsthand history may yet be found. The work will have to go on without Michael Ventris. The young man, whose achievement was hailed by R. D. Barnett of the British Museum as "the Everest of Greek archaeology," was killed in an automobile accident in 1956. Ventris was only thirty-four at the time, but he accomplished a feat that makes his life and career forever memorable. I. J. Gelb called it, "the most successful single attempt in the whole history of the decipherment of unknown writings and languages." Coming from a scholar famous for his own work as a decipherer, this is high praise indeed for an amateur.

Chapter Fifteen

Languages Lost and Found

I

A French general dreams of a new world empire and invades Egypt; a British soldier and diplomat has himself lowered down the carved face of a mountain to copy inscriptions; a German schoolteacher makes a bet, and an eleven-year-old makes a vow; findings that inspire the work of countless scholars are made by a doctor, an architect, and a banknote engraver. The story of the discovery and decipherment of lost languages is filled with incredible color and drama. The search for clues and the puzzling out of these mysterious languages have revealed the existence of whole civilizations forgotten and lost in the passing of centuries. Deciphering the lost languages has demonstrated the underlying truth of numerous legends that were long considered more fiction than fact. The decipherers, amateur and expert alike, have

172

contributed enormously to the knowledge gained by the science of archaeology.

Less dramatic, but of considerable interest to scholars, is the problem of how languages are "lost" to begin with. The destruction of a city or an empire need not mean that the language spoken there is equally destroyed. The Acropolis and the Forum are ruins in modern Athens and Rome, but the languages of classical Greece and the Roman Empire are still read today. Nevertheless, the decay or destruction of a culture is usually accompanied by the loss of its language. Sometimes that loss is gradual. The Sumerians were vanquished, but their language was taken over and adapted by the Semites who conquered them. The resulting cuneiform writing survived the fall of Babylon and Nineveh to be used by the Persians. In time, however, even Old Persian cuneiform disappeared from use.

Linear A was presumably supplanted by Linear B as the Minoan civilization developed. Linear B, however, appears to have been abandoned by the early Greeks in favor of the Phoenician script. Some languages are transformed, and some are discarded; others may be said to atrophy. Egyptian hieroglyphics remained in use after the development of demotic writing, but that use became more and more specialized. Though fewer people knew its use in Greco-Roman times, hieroglyphics continued to serve Egyptian priests, as it had done for 3,000 years. But the advantages of an alphabetic script were apparent, and hieroglyphics had never developed along alphabetic lines.

173

As the people who used them disappeared, as better systems came along, the old languages died. Not all the vanished languages are beyond recall. If it was written, as well as spoken, and especially if it produced a worthwhile literature, a lost language left the means for its own recovery. As long as records of a language are available, they are sure to be studied by scholars.

If both the language and its system of writing are known, decipherment is no problem; if both the language and writing are unknown, decipherment may be impossible. Decipherment is easier when a language is known and the writing is not than when the writing is known but the language is not. Consider two cases: A friend sends you a message in which every letter has been replaced by a symbol; an Oriental visitor to the United Nations picks up a printed circular. In the first case, though the writing is strange to you, you have the advantage of knowing that the message is in English. In the second case, though the visitor may recognize the letters of the Latin alphabet, he knows that English, Spanish, French, Italian, German, and even Turkish use this alphabet. The cuneiform scholars, as in the second case, faced a situation where different languages shared the same system of writing.

In general, the methods employed by scholars of lost languages are like those used by cryptographers. The cryptographic technique relies on probable word and letter combinations for clues. These clues require an understanding of the language—familiarity with vowel placement, methods of pluralization, grammatical structure, and common word endings among other things. For instance, in working out an English language cryptogram, a letter or symbol standing alone is most apt to be an *I* or an *A;* a frequently appearing three-letter word is probably "and" or "the"; many consonants can be doubled, but of the vowels only *e* and *o* are likely; *ing* and *ed* are common present and past tense word endings; and superlatives are usually expressed by the *est* ending. Then, too, "?he" may be "the" or "she," but "t?e" is almost certainly "the," rather than "toe."

Proper names provide decipherers with major aids. Champollion's key clues were the names of Ptolemy and Cleopatra. Another aid is the traditional title, such as King of Kings, which Grotefend used to advantage. The royal inscriptions that the early decipherers studied, such as that on Behistun, were filled with names, titles, and, equally helpful, lists of countries or cities. These inscriptions are stylized and not idiomatic in the modern sense. It is perhaps fortunate for the scholars that they did not have to work with contemporary American English.

There is something that remains tentative even in fully deciphered languages—pronunciation. Scholars who can read and write ancient languages fluently cannot speak them with equal ease. For instance, the ancient Egyptians omitted vowels when writing, and modern scholars can never really be certain how the vowel sounds were pronounced. The clues a scholar relies on are more helpful in the study of a written language than in its spoken form.

175

II

However a language may be lost, finding it again depends on its written record. The most durable writing material, and one of the most widely used, has been stone. The ancient Egyptians, who wrote on papyrus, and the Babylonians, who used a wedgelike stylus on wet clay, also carved messages in stone. Long before them, men were leaving their record on stone, the earliest writing material we know of. In Spain and France there are caves that were lived in more than 10,000 years ago. We know this because Paleolithic man drew on the walls of these caves. These drawings mark not only the beginning of art, but also the recording of events, and may be considered the earliest form of writing.

The earliest writing, in a stricter sense of the term, was undoubtedly pictorial. In this kind of writing a picture of a dog meant dog, and a circle meant sun. This picture writing developed into a system using ideographs or ideograms (word-signs). Now the symbol represented an idea associated with the pictured object; an eye, for example, meant see. In this writing a circle could mean day, one step removed from sun, and later interpreters would have to puzzle out such difficulties.

The next step, the development of phonetic writing, grew out of the lack of relation between the pictured object and the spoken name for it. Phonetic writing began somewhat in the form of the rebus (see page 65). Ancient Egyptian hieroglyphics combined phonograms

176

(sound-signs) and ideograms (sense-signs), using two sizes of symbols to differentiate between them. There were two kinds of phonogram: the polyphonic, representing more than one sound, and the homophonic. Homophones had the same phonetic value but stood for different objects. The ancient Egyptians never completely replaced sense-signs with sound-signs, and hieroglyphics remained picturc writing assistcd by sound-signs.

In Mesopotamia a form of writing developed in which symbols stood for syllables. From this syllabic script there developed an alphabetic system of signs representing single sounds. There were more than twenty of these, all representing consonants. Because no vowels were written, the sign for *wa* could also represent *we, wi* or *wu,* depending on the context in which it appeared.

The Greeks, by way of the Phoenicians, borrowed the idea of an alphabet from its Semitic originators. These origins can be seen in a comparison of the Greek *alpha, beta, gamma, delta . . .* with the Semitic *aleph, beth, gimel, daleth. . . .* The Greeks added vowels and other improvements, including writing from left to right. At first they experimented with the boustrophedon system, writing alternate lines from right to left and then from left to right. The simplest but best explanation for settling on a left-to-right system is that it is most suited to a right handed person writing with a pen.

The Romans gained their alphabet, the one we use, from the Etruscans. They borrowed twenty-one of the Etruscans' twenty-six letters: A B C D E F Z H I K L M

177

N O P Q R S T V X. Slowly this alphabet developed into the one with which we are familiar. First the *Z*, which had the sound of a *g* or *k,* was replaced by *G.* Later *Y* and *Z* were added at the end, taken from the Greeks to aid in writing borrowed Greek texts. This twenty-three-letter alphabet was the one used in imperial Rome. In the tenth century the *V* was expanded into *U* and *W* (double *U*), and four centuries later the differentiation between *I* and *J* was introduced.

In picture writing, thousands of different signs may be needed; an alphabetic system requires relatively few signs. This wonderful advance carried one drawback with it. Because letters originated as phonetic symbols, any reader in ancient times could probably pronounce an unfamiliar word at sight. This is not true today. In using the Roman alphabet, which developed by adapting to the requirements of various different languages, we are forced to make do with an inadequate system. In English, twenty-six letters represent forty-seven phonemes, the sounds that make up a language. We have twelve vowel sounds, twenty-six consonant sounds, and nine dipthongs, resorting to combinations of letters such as *ch, sh,* or *th* to represent some sounds and giving more than one sound to some letters. Trying to spell some English words correctly teaches us the price we have to pay for progress.

III

The permanence of stone records has contributed to

the rescuing from oblivion of more than one lost language. It has also left modern scholars with more than one unsolved puzzle, for not all the lost languages have been deciphered. Throughout the world, silent stones in a variety of languages await their Champollions.

Some of these undeciphered scripts clearly bear a relation to languages that have given up their secrets to the decipherers. Linear A is one, along with the hieroglyphic writing that first drew Evans to Crete. The seal stones that attracted his attention and the dozen samples of Linear A he uncovered at Knossos have been supplemented by findings at Hagia Triada. The Linear A samples are known to be inventories, and three classes of signs (ideograms, syllabograms, and word dividers) have been identified. But Linear A remains a puzzle.

The writing on the Phaistos Disk bears some resemblances to Cretan writing, but its differences suggest that it represents an independent system. The mystery of its "printed" characters remains unsolved, and it seems unlikely that the language contains only the forty-five signs of the disk. The other supposed clue to Cretan writing, the Cypriot script, has not yielded up all its mysteries. That syllabary, used to write Greek but not well suited to the purpose, had been designed originally for a local language, now called Eteocyprian. Analysis of this earlier language has revealed something of its structure, but more samples are needed to really understand it.

There are about 10,000 known samples of Etruscan writing, but the language cannot be understood. Attempts

179

at decipherment date back to the first century B.C. It was then considered a language unlike any other, and modern scholars have come no closer to relating it to any known language. The most helpful clues have been some identifiable paintings with accompanying names and a pair of dice found in a tomb. The dice have provided the names of the numbers one to six, but it is not certain that these numbers were arranged by the Etruscans as they are on modern dice.

Other clues to the riddle of Etruscan have been more disappointing than revealing. Thirty brief Etrusco-Latin bilingual inscriptions have not proved helpful, except in the translation of some brief texts. Several words have been worked out, but the long inscriptions have defied translation. More than 500 different words have been noted, but not deciphered, in long inscriptions found on linen mummy wrappings. This macabre note is typical of the study of Etruscan, for well over three-quarters of the inscriptions we have are funerary. There is no evidence of an Etruscan literature; just epitaphs, tomb inscriptions, mummy wrappings, and little else—except a mystery more than 2,000 years old.

Another undeciphered language related to a known one is Proto-Elamite. The early version of this writing appears to have been ideographic, containing several hundred signs. It came into use, perhaps 5,000 years ago, at Susa, the capital of ancient Elam. The later script, which seems to have contained as few as sixty signs, was apparently abandoned for a form of cuneiform. The development and evolution of these scripts, from Susian ideographs to the Elamite cuneiform of the Rock of Behistun, requires much more study before all their secrets are revealed. That study will undoubtedly involve the Sumerian and Babylonian neighbors of the Elamites.

Farther east, in the Indus Valley, a civilization arose about 2,500 B.C. and flourished for 1,000 years. Its existence has been known for little over a century, and detailed study of it dates from the 1920's. The writing of this civilization, mainly ideographic, has been preserved in the form of copper and stone seals. About 800 of these have been found, and it is believed that any other writing must have been done on less durable materials. Attempts have been made to link the language with those of the Mesopotamians and the Hittites. A relation has even been suggested to the *rongo rongo* script of Easter Island. But the language of the Indus Valley people remains a mystery, as much a mystery as the people themselves.

When Easter Island was discovered in 1722, one of the world's most fascinating puzzles came to light. The strange gigantic statues distributed over the tiny island have fascinated people ever since. The mystery that surrounded them has overshadowed the equally mysterious writing found there, but nowhere else in Polynesia. Few samples remain of this pictographic script, called *kohau-rongo-rongo* by the natives. Some if its symbols are geometric designs; others depict humans, fish, birds, and plants. The natives said the inscriptions were charms, but even in 1722 no one could read them. Theories have been put forward suggesting that the writing was imported from China or the Indus Valley. It may have been brought to the island in the twelfth century, as local tradition maintains, but from where is still uncertain.

A lost language of the Western world, that of the Mayas, was deliberately destroyed through the fanaticism of one man. The Spanish Bishop of Yucatán, intent on wiping out the native religion, ordered the destruction of all Mayan records shortly after the conquest of Mexico. Only three out of hundreds of manuscripts survived his zealous attack. Ironically, a forgotten book of his, discovered in the nineteenth century in the Royal Library of Madrid, discussed the Mayan glyphs in detail. A Mayan alphabet contained in the book proved incorrect and useless, but other information in the book supplied scholars with worthwhile clues. For the bishop had not destroyed the many monumental inscriptions found by later explorers in the jungle-covered Mayan ruins.

About one-third of the Mayan glyphs have been assigned meanings. The system of writing seems to be mainly ideographic. Though some scholars feel it contains phonetic elements, I. J. Gelb has argued against this. A phonetic writing, where the language is known, says Gelb, should not remain indecipherable. The Mayan language is known and continues to be spoken in Yucatán. Because the writing remains undeciphered, Gelb is convinced that it cannot be phonetic. Logic, at least, seems to be on his side.

And so the story of lost languages has no final chapter. Some of the languages will no doubt remain mysteries. Others require more samples for study before they give up their secrets. Work is progressing on the partially deciphered scripts. New discoveries may bring fascinating revelations. The slightest clue can provide a key to the hardest puzzle. The forgotten languages of the ancient world lay buried for centuries, yet from Champollion to Ventris is a span of two lifetimes. With the technology available to modern scholars, what will another lifetime bring? Decipherment goes on.

Suggestions for Further Reading

For anyone developing an interest in archaeology, the best first book on the subject, and probably also the most popular, is: *Gods, Graves, and Scholars: The Story of Archaeology,* by C. W. Ceram. New York, Alfred A. Knopf, 1967. 2d rev. ed.

A supplement to this is a volume that is primarily a picture book: *The March of Archaeology,* by C. W. Ceram. New York, Alfred A. Knopf, 1958.

On the subject of decipherment, an excellent book is: *Lost Languages,* by P. E. Cleator. New York, John Day Company, 1959. (Also available in paperback: Mentor Books, 1962.)

More anecdotal, but not as clear, is: *Voices in Stone: The Decipherment of Ancient Scripts and Writings,* by Ernst Doblhofer. New York, Viking Press, 1961.

And for a detailed account of the work done in one area, there is the authoritative: *The Decipherment of Linear B,* by John Chadwick. New York, Vintage Books, 1963.

The original writings of the great archaelogists may be sampled in three anthologies:

The Treasures of Time: Firsthand Accounts by Famous Archaeologists of Their Work in the Near East, selected, edited and introduced by Leo Deuel. Cleveland, World Publishing Company, 1961.

Hands on the Past: Pioneer Archaeologists Tell Their Own Story, edited by C. W. Ceram. New York, Alfred A. Knopf, 1966.

The World of the Past, edited, with an introduction and introductory notes by Jacquetta Hawkes. New York, Alfred A. Knopf, 1963. 2 vol.

There are many very readable accounts of the early civilizations, though not all of them deal with the decipherment of their languages.

On the subject of Crete, a good popular book is: *The Bull of Minos,* by Leonard Cottrell. New York, Rinehart & Company, 1958.

A comprehensive introduction to Mesopotamia is: *Ancient Semitic Civilizations,* by Sabatino Moscati. New York, Capricorn Books, 1960.

Of the many books on ancient Egypt and its archaeology, one to start with is: *Everyday Life in Ancient Egypt,* by Jon Manchip White. New York, G. P. Putnam's Sons, 1963.

A brief but exciting account of Napoleon's campaign is contained in: *The Blue Nile,* by Alan Moorehead. New York, Harper & Row, 1962.

It is covered in greater detail, along with a full account of the Institute of Egypt, in: *Bonaparte in Egypt,* by J. Christopher Herold. New York, Harper & Row, 1962.

Two books in the series *Great Ages of Man* should be mentioned for their combination of readable texts and absolutely superb illustrations. They are:

Ancient Egypt, by Lionel Casson & Editors of Time-Life Books. New York, Time Inc., 1965.

Cradle of Civilization, by Samuel Noah Kramer & Editors of Time-Life Books. New York, Time Inc., 1967.

Glossary

Most of the technical or specialized terms in this book are explained as they appear. Some others are explained below, particularly as they relate to the book.

Alabaster—a variety of gypsum (*see* Gypsum), usually white, used for ornaments.

Antiquities—remains from ancient times, such as relics or monuments.

Basalt—dark rock formed from lava flows.

Brush proofs—copies made by brushing layers of wet paper over inscribed (or raised) surfaces; when dry and peeled off, they serve as molds for plaster or other copies.

Cabalistic—pertaining to the Cabala, mystic and occult Hebrew writings of the Middle Ages.

Calcined—oxidized by heating or burning.

Configuration—the disposition or arrangement of the parts of a thing; the actual form taken by the arranged parts.

Consonantal—pertaining to consonant sounds, as opposed to vowel sounds.

Cryptographer—one who studies secret writing, especially codes and ciphers.

Cursive—in flowing strokes resembling handwriting.

Declension—the inflection (*see* Inflection) of words for categories such as case and number.

Dig—the informal term for an archaeological site being excavated.

Diphthong—a mixed or gliding, but nevertheless single, speech sound; written so as to show its apparent components (as in *ch* or *oi*).

Glyph—a pictograph (*see* Pictograph) or hieroglyph; technically a carving.

Gypsum—a common mineral, soft and chalklike, used for making plaster of Paris.

Hellenistic—pertaining to the Greeks and their culture after the time of Alexander the Great.

Homonym—a word like another in sound and spelling but different in meaning (as "bear," meaning to carry, and "bear," the animal); differs from *homophone* in that homophones may be spelled differently (as in "bear" and "bare").

Hypothesis—a proposition or assumption (even a guess) set forth to explain the occurrence of specific phenomena.

Ideographic—pertaining to ideographs or ideograms, written symbols representing objects or ideas rather than word or speech sounds.

Incised—cut into; made by cutting.

Inflectional—pertaining to inflection (as an inflectional ending); adding to or changing the shape of a base word to give it a different function (as adding *s* for a plural or *ed* for the past tense). *See* Paradigms.

Interpolator—one who alters a text by adding new material, usually without authority to do so and often incorrectly.

Linguistics—the science of language.

Neolithic—pertaining to the later part of the Stone Age.

Orientalist—one who studies the Orient, which, in the early days of archaeology, more often meant the Near East than the Far East, as it does now.

Paleography—the study of ancient writing.

Paleolithic—the period of the Stone Age that preceded the Neolithic.

Paradigms—sets of all the inflected forms of single elements; also examples, patterns or models.

Paraphrase—a rewording or restatement of a text giving the meaning in another (sometimes clearer) form.

Phoneme—any one of the set of basic units of sound by which words or parts of words are represented.

Phonetic—pertaining to speech sounds or their transcription in written symbols.

Pictographic—the use of pictorial signs or symbols in a written record or inscription.

Script—the letters or characters used in handwriting; a system of writing (*see* Cursive).

Stele—a stone slab or pillar bearing an inscription, usually a monument or a marker.

Stratum—a naturally or artificially formed layer of material, usually one of a series of parallel layers, or strata.

Stylus—a pointed instrument for writing, most familiarly a pen.

Syllabary—a set of written symbols, each representing a syllable, rather than a single sound, used to write certain languages.

Tell—an artificial mound made up of the accumulated remains of ancient settlements; in the Near East often part of a place-name.

Transliteration—the change that takes place when rewriting letters or words of one alphabet or language in corresponding characters of another alphabet or language (not to be confused with "translation"—rendering something written or spoken from one language into another).

Vestiges—visible traces of something no longer present or existing.

Index

Abraham, 122
Abukir Bay, 23, 25, 26
Abydos, Royal List of, 71
Adad, 79
Akkad, 76, 122
Aleppo, 111
Alexander the Great, 36, 54, 71
Alexandria, 15, 17, 21, 23, 26, 88, 107
Amarna, Tell el, 132, 133
Amenhotep III, 11
Anquetil-Dupperon, Abraham Hyacinthe, 91, 96
Anu, 79
Aram, 75
Ariadne, 148
Armenia, 73
Artaxerxes, 95
Arzawa, 133, 134
Ashmolean Museum, 150, 155
Ashur, 79
Ashurbanipal (Sardanapalus), 77, 121
Ashurnasirpal II, 77, 116
Asshur, 75
Assyria, 74, 76, 77, 79, 83, 84, 121, 132
Athens, 147, 173
Awad, 113

Babel, Tower of, 129
Babylon, 9, 76, 77, 79, 82, 85, 98, 103, 127–29, 131, 173
Babylonia, 74, 76, 77, 82, 83, 93, 121, 124, 127, 132
Baghdad, 98, 101, 111
Bankes, W. J., 50
Barnett, R. D., 171
Bauer, Hans, 145
Bedouins, 16, 19, 23
Behistun, 87, 99, 100, 102–4, 120, 127, 162, 175, 181
Benjamin of Tudela, 88
Bennett, E. L., 164, 165
Berthollet, Claude Louis, 27, 28, 29
Bible, 75, 77, 80, 81, 110, 126
Black Sea, 9, 76
Blegen, C. W., 164, 169

Bogazköy, 133, 134, 136, 139, 141
Bolzani, G. V. P., 37
Bonaparte, Napoleon, 13, 14, 15, 20, 22–29, 31, 33, 49, 90
Bossert, Helmuth T., 141, 142
Botta, Paul Émile, 107–10, 116, 117, 120
Bouchard, Captain, 31
British Museum, 35, 98, 104, 116, 125, 126, 171
British School of Archaeology (Athens), 152
Brueys, Admiral, 25
Brun, Cornelias le, 90
Burckhardt, Johann Ludwig, 132
Burnouf, Eugène, 96, 99, 103
Burton, Sir Richard, 133

Caffarelli, François Marie Auguste, 27
Cairo, 13, 15, 16, 17–18, 23, 24, 25, 29, 30, 31, 89
Cambyses, 95
Canaanites, 143, 144
Canning, Sir Stratford, 112
Cape Fennel (Ras Shamra), 144, 145
Capitol (Rome), 12
Carchemish, 132
Chadwick, John, 165
Champollion, Jean François, 40, 44, 45, 46–59, 63, 70, 97, 161, 175, 183
Champollion-Figeac, Jacques Joseph, 47, 48, 49, 59
Chardin, Jean (Sir John), 89–90
Cleopatra, 36, 51, 52, 97, 175
Colossi of Memnon, 11
Constantinople, 88, 112, 116, 134
Conté, Nicolas Jacques, 28, 31
Copts, 37
Crete, 146–58, 162, 163, 169, 179
Cyrus, 77, 93, 95

Daedalus, 148
Damietta, 15
Darius, 88, 95, 96, 99, 100, 102, 119

189

Darwin, Charles, 124
Dendera, 57–58
Denon, Dominique Vivant, 28, 33
Dhautpoul, 31
Dhorme, Édouard, 145
Dolomieu, Déodat Guy Silvain Tancrede Gratet de, 28
Dussaud, René, 143

East India Company, 98, 101
Easter Island, 181–82
Eber, 75
Eden, 126
Egypt, 7–18, 21, 22, 24, 26, 28–30, 33, 36–37, 49, 54, 57, 58, 61, 70, 71, 72, 73, 77, 86, 107, 110, 131, 154
Elam, 120
Elvand, Mount, 101, 103
Embaba, 24
Enki (Ea), 79
Enkidu, 81
Enlil, 79
Etemenanki, 85
Etruscans, 177, 179–80
Euphrates, 73, 103, 111
Evans, Sir Arthur, 149–59, 162, 163, 168, 179
Ezbekiah, 17

Flandin, Eugène Napoléon, 109
Flower, Samuel, 90, 91
Forrer, Emil, 139
Fourier, Jean Baptiste Joseph, 28, 31, 47
Francis I, 14

Galland, Citizen, 31
Gelb, I. J., 139, 171, 182
Geoffroy Saint-Hilaire, Étienne, 28, 34
Gilgamesh, 81, 82, 117, 125–26, 141, 160
Grenoble, University of, 47, 48, 49, 50
Grotefend, Georg F., 93–98, 101, 104, 125, 130, 175

Hagia Triada, 179
Halbherr, Federigo, 152
Hama, 132, 133, 134, 135

Hammurabi, 76, 82, 141
Hanging Gardens, 129
Harmakhis, 8
Hathor, 58
Hatti, 131, 132, 134
Helffrich, Johannes, 12
Herodotus, 9–11, 12, 40, 73, 74, 96, 127, 128
Hincks, Edward, 104, 105, 106, 121
Hittites, 76, 131–32, 133–35, 141
Hogarth, D. G., 152
Holtzmann, Adolf, 104
Horapollon, 38, 39
Hrozný, Bedřich, 136–37, 138, 139
Hutchinson, John H., 34
Hystaspes, 95, 96

Ibrahim Bey, 20, 24
India, 83, 89, 101, 105
Indus Valley, 181, 182
Institute of Egypt, 28–31, 32, 34
Iraq, 74
Ishtar, 79, 81
Isis, 58

Jomard, Edmé François, 30

Kämpfer, Engelbert, 90
Kara Tepe, 141, 142
Karnak, Royal Tablet of, 71
Kephala, 149, 150
Kermanshah, 101, 102
Khafre, 8
Khorsabad, 108–9, 113, 115
Kircher, Athanasius, 38
Kléber, Jean Baptiste, 33
Knossos, 147, 148, 149, 151, 152, 155, 156, 158, 163, 165, 167, 169, 179
Knudzton, J. A., 133
Kober, Alice, 166, 167
Koldewey, Robert, 127–29
Kuyunjik, 105, 107, 116, 126

Lancret, Citizen, 31
Lassen, Christian, 96, 99, 103
Lavoisier, Antoine, 27
Layard, Austen Henry, 107, 110–17, 120, 121, 126, 127, 130
Lenoir, Alexandre, 48
Lepsius, Karl R., 59

190

The Author

STEVEN FRIMMER is the managing editor of a major New York publishing house. He has been an actor, advertising copywriter, and a book club director. Mr. Frimmer lives with his wife and three daughters in a house on the edge of the New Jersey Meadows, where he practices such hobbies as keeping the house in one piece and reading books on archaeology.